UNPOPULAR RELIGION

UNPOPULAR RELIGION

A CLARIFICATION OF CHRISTIANITY

ERIK SWENSON

INDEPENDENT PUBLISHER

Copyright © 2013, 2018 by Erik Swenson. Text revised in 2018.
All rights reserved. Applies to text, illustrations, and photographs.

Published by IM PRESS
A division of Incarnate Ministries
www.incarnateministries.com

All rights reserved. No part of this publication may be reproduced by any means—for example, electronic, photocopy, recording—without prior written permission of the publisher.

ISBN 10: 1-7323-2320-8
ISBN 978-1-7323-2320-9

All Scripture quotations, unless otherwise indicated, are taken from the Holy Bible New International Version (NIV). Copyright © 1973, 1978, 1984 by International Bible Society. Used by permission of Zondervan. All rights reserved.

Because of the dynamic nature of the Internet, any web addresses or links contained in this book may have changed since publication.

To Heather, my lily among the thorns

CONTENTS

Author's note

Introduction

Part I Intolerant
1: Shoes Laced with Explosives
2: Weatherman
3: You'll Put Your Eye Out
4: The Invisible Elephant

Part II Irrational
5: Mud People
6: Infinity Plus One
7: Small Next to God
8: Don't Eat Sand

Part III Irrelevant
9: Go Back to Your Own Neighborhood
10: Jack Fell Down
11: Killed but Not Dead
12: The Fog Burned Up

Afterword

Acknowledgments

Notes

AUTHOR'S NOTE

This is a book about Christianity.

It was a hard book to write for a few reasons. One, Christianity is a massive topic. Where do you begin? What is the angle? People have written entire books about a single passage in the Bible. In addition, there are countless denominations—each with a different take.

Second, there are a million books about Christianity. What is there to add to the discussion? How do you avoid getting lost in the loud dialogue? It feels kind of like the day I got lost at the Minnesota state fair. I was two feet shorter than everyone else. All I could see were legs moving frantically, carrying with them the smell of corn dogs.

But the main reason this was a difficult book is that Christianity is not popular. As we will see, negative perceptions of this religion abound.

It would have been far easier to write a book about a something else. Take polyurethane foam, for example. That would be a good choice for a book. It is a narrow topic, you are not likely to find many listings on Amazon, and I am not aware of anyone opposed to it. Who doesn't like foam? Everyone uses foam. It is in everything from bike helmets to surfboards, and if you drive a car, you sit on it every day.

But the reality is, there is not any point in writing a book if you are not going to actually say something. So at the risk of becoming unpopular, I went with Christianity.

This is me joining a conversation that has been underway for a long time. I ask you to test these words. I am fully aware the topic I've selected is vast and the conclusions about it are varied. But I also know with everything I am that this is the most important conversation I could ever be a part of.

I invite you to join me.

INTRODUCTION

Christianity is an unpopular religion.

I need to begin by defining those terms. Unpopular simply means unfavorable or disliked. Religion is a more difficult word because it has a history. For many it is a negative word. Atheist author Christopher Hitchens told us, "Religion poisons everything." Political comedian Bill Maher suggested the answer to ending violence is not to ban guns but to ban religion. In these cases, the reference to religion is a general one but it includes Christianity. Many Jesus followers resist the idea of Christianity being classified as a religion because of the negative connotations linked to the word. My intention is to use it in a neutral manner if possible. I am simply referring to a set of beliefs about God that tend to unify a group of people. In this sense, the belief there are a million gods is a religious belief. The belief there is one God who came to save and initiate a relationship with human beings is also a religious belief. And I would even say the belief that God does not exist is a religious belief (or at least a religious position). It is possible I am assigning an oversimplified definition of the word. But this is all I mean to say when I use it.

It may seem odd to classify Christianity as unpopular considering it is one of the major world religions. There are billions of people who ascribe to Christianity. If popularity is judged by the size of the following (and usually it is) it would seem more logical to classify this religion as popular. But although there are a large number of people who follow Christianity, there are also a large number of people who don't. There are more people who live outside this belief system than inside it.

The degree of unpopularity varies depending on the situation. In many nations, Christians are violently persecuted. This reality is often ignored, but the persecution is real. While this is a vital topic, it is not the topic of this book. A helpful discussion of the persecuted church would require many volumes, and those who have worn chains and run from bullets would be far more qualified to speak about it.

In this book I intend to look at look at views of Christianity that range from indifference to annoyance. When we speak about negative perceptions of this religion in America, they usually fall into one of those categories. Allow me to expand.

The book *Christian America?* by Christian Smith addresses perceptions of evangelical Christians in America. In introducing his study, Smith's book refers to the fact that Christianity has become, for many Americans, a "worrisome part of this country's cultural and political landscape." Smith also quoted Curtis Wilkie of the *Boston Globe*, who described born-again or fundamentalist Christians as an "invisible army."[1]

Lee Strobel, author of *The Case for the Real Jesus*, cited an exercise conducted by Jon Meacham and Sally Quinn on the *Newsweek* website in which people were asked to provide their thoughts on who the real Jesus was. The responses were varied, but one comment revealed several rather common perceptions of Christians: "Jesus is a fairy tale for grown-ups. Unfortunately, he's a fairy tale that leads people to bomb clinics, despise women, denigrate reason, and embrace greed."[2]

After conducting a three-year study on perceptions of Christianity held by those outside the church, David Kinnaman concluded quite simply that this religion has a major "image problem." He found that many in the younger generations have "little trust in the Christian faith" and view Christianity as "weary and threadbare."[3]

Some are even more resolved in their mistrust of Christianity. Sam Harris, in his book *Letter to a Christian Nation*, skipped over reservation and went directly to overt rejection. He referred to the Bible as categorically "false" and stated that the Christian beliefs held by many Americans equate to a "moral and intellectual emergency."[4]

Popular culture echoes the sentiments referenced above. Over the past decades the creative minds of our country have provided a very recognizable caricature of Christianity. There was the sweater-wearing, mustache-growing Ned Flanders who served as the moral guardrail for Homer Simpson. *South Park* gave us a waddling paper cutout of Jesus. Phil Hartman of *Saturday Night Live* appeared as Jesus in a white robe to the woman praying for an open parking stall. In the movie *RV*, Robin Williams listened impatiently as a bubbly southern woman relayed the story of how Jesus saved her from a tornado by sliding an old mattress out to break her fall. Collectively we find a religion that seems easily dismissed and good for a laugh (although I will admit the tornado story was pretty funny).

While all of this is telling, the best example I could provide is the young girl I saw walking into the public library. She had on a black T-shirt with a large emblem on the front that looked like a no smoking sign; but the cigarette was replaced with a Christian cross. The words "Bad Religion" spanned across the top.

In short, there is a vast and general distaste for Christianity—but it is not helpful to talk in vast and general terms. We need to be more specific in identifying the negative perceptions of this religion. There are many of them, actually. In this book, I would like to look at three that I believe are widespread.

1. CHRISTIANS ARE INTOLERANT

Christianity is viewed as a religion of intolerance. It is seen as a place where self-righteous people gather to pass out judgment and build walls. Lee Strobel summarized this idea well when he wrote, "Christianity's claim to being the only way to God is vehemently branded as the height of religious intolerance."[5] In the study conducted by David Kinnaman (referenced above) it was determined there are tens of millions of young Americans who reside "outside" of Christianity. Of this demographic, 91 percent believe Christians to be antihomosexual, 87 percent view Christians as judgmental, and 85 percent find Christians to be hypocritical.[6] One respondent said, "Most people I meet assume that Christian means very conservative, entrenched in their thinking, anti-gay, anti-choice, angry, violent, illogical, empire builders; they want to convert everyone and they generally cannot live peacefully with anyone who doesn't believe what they believe." Kinnaman concluded the overwhelming perception that Christians are intolerant comes from the fact that the church is known primarily for what it stands against. He said, "We have become famous for what we oppose, rather than who we are for."[7]

2) CHRISTIANS ARE IRRATIONAL

Many hold the Christian faith to be irrational. It is seen as unreasonable to believe God became a man—or that God exists at all. To suggest that God created the universe is scientific blasphemy. Atheist Sam Harris has pointed out that the United States ranks thirty-third out of thirty-four nations in terms of the percentage of the population that accepts Darwinism (or evolution). He connects this statistic to the fact that students in the United States fall below almost all of Europe and Asia in understanding of science and math. His conclusion is simple. He said, "These data are unequivocal: we are building a civilization of ignorance."[8] Harris is just one of many vocal intellectuals who present the Christian world-view as something to be mocked by any serious, rational person. Among his contemporaries is the charismatic Richard Dawkins, who offered the world a massive volume dedicated to his belief that God is no more than a delusion.

3) CHRISTIANITY IS IRRELEVANT

People have come to see the Christian gospel as irrelevant. In a world that feels terminally ill, Christians carry on about eternity but seem to have little hope to offer those beaten down and bloodied by suffering here and now. In the *Newsweek* survey cited previously, one respondent wrote, "Honestly, I don't care about Jesus. Who or what he was, is or isn't doesn't affect me."[9] In the book *A Million Miles in a Thousand Years*, Donald Miller told the story of his friend Kathy, who traveled to Rwanda. While there she visited a church that had housed a crowd of people trying to escape the genocide. The bones and skulls of the victims remain there as a memorial. Miller said his friend turned to God in response to this and prayed, "See, you created us only to let us march around in our own misery. You are supposed to be good. What are you good for?"[10]

Intolerant, irrational, and irrelevant—this is the perception of Christianity in America. In response to this disapproval, I find Christians often react in one of two ways. In order to illustrate, we need to consider the difference between a foam dart and a paintball.

When I was a kid we used to play with Nerf guns. In other words, we found a safe way to shoot things. This sounds simple until you understand that the Nerf gun is not a perfect machine. The trigger releases a puff that sends a foam dart twirling through the air. Imagine throwing a cotton ball in the wind. My brother and I did improve the performance by wrapping the darts in duct tape to add weight and create a pressure buildup in the barrel. But that is cheating. The foam dart by itself leaves minimal impact on an intended target, if it reaches the target at all. (I should acknowledge that foam dart technology has improved vastly in the twenty-five years since I was a kid—but hopefully I can still salvage the metaphor).

It wasn't until I was older that I realized foam darts were wimpy. The revelation came when some neighborhood kids invited me to play paintball. I put on a thin flannel shirt and jeans and met them in the woods.

A paintball gun contains a highly pressurized CO_2 cartridge that discharges a solid pellet similar to a lead musket ball. The ammo is hurled with such raw force that when it strikes human flesh, the recipient will literally believe the shot came from a real gun (especially if wearing a thin flannel shirt). The only difference is that the bullet does not penetrate the skin. Instead it beats against the body and splatters, leaving a massive, raised welt.

When Christians sense their faith is under attack, one option is to conform—go quiet, drop convictions, make adjustments to one's beliefs, or abandon them all together. As a result, this type of Christianity is not able to make much of an impact on the world. I call it *Foam Dart Christianity*. The other option is to move in the opposite direction—separate, take up arms, identify the enemies of the faith and defend Christianity fiercely. This type of Christianity leaves welts. I call it *Paintball Christianity*. I can actually fully relate to both reactions because I have lived in both places. I also believe that in many cases, the motives behind these responses generally start out good.

With *Foam Dart Christianity*, the goal is to reconcile this religion to the culture. This approach recognizes that Christians have made huge mistakes and seeks not only to apologize for these sins but also to avoid recreating them in the future. This is a good thing.

Paintball Christianity interprets this disapproval from the culture as a weight bearing down on and threatening to crush the religion. The gut response when one's deep beliefs are being attacked is to passionately defend them—especially if the criticism seems unfounded. This is understandable. So both reactions make sense. But if we only live in one extreme or the other, things become unbalanced and distorted.

A follower of *Foam Dart Christianity* may begin to apologize for everything, validating any and every criticism and conforming to every popular opinion. The goal, then, becomes seeking acceptance rather than reconciliation—even if that means abandoning convictions all together. There is a well-known bishop by the name of John Shelby Spong who wrote a book called *Why Christianity Must Change or Die: A Bishop Speaks to Believers in Exile*. From what I understand, this man has dedicated himself to reversing much of the judgmental and intolerant behavior displayed by so many Christian organizations and individuals. I find his striving for reconciliation to be very noble. But in his attempt to bring reconciliation, it appears he has largely abandoned many of the foundational beliefs of the Christian religion. I am not judging his decision. I am just suggesting that his belief system represents something other than traditional Christianity. Here are the assertions of his book.

- Traditional theism is no longer credible. We need a new, contemporary understanding of God as the source of life and love, not as a superperson running the universe.

- Jesus can no longer be the incarnation of a theistic deity.

- Heaven and hell don't exist.[11]

The power in the Christian message comes from the fact that death and hell are real and that there is a God who dove into the deep caverns of hell to rescue us and pull us out. Remove that and the power of the message is gone. It is just air passing through our lips.

A disciple of *Paintball Christianity* can become so focused on promoting the superiority of Christianity that he or she refuses to even hear the critics or to acknowledge mistakes. These believers are seeking not to preserve their Christianity, but to wield it as a blunt object with which to beat the competition. In the introduction of his *Letter to a Christian Nation*, Harris talked about the piles of mail he receives from people telling him he is wrong not to believe in God. He stated the most "hostile" rebukes come from Christians. He knows this because they "always cite chapter and verse."[12] Now, Harris is no novice with a gun and is not afraid to fire his own harsh criticisms. But the point is, this same type of retaliation is somewhat common among Christians.

I would like to suggest a third option. It involves borrowing tactics from both sides. This is not a compromise. It is actually more difficult to live in some sort of balance between these two extremes. It involves acknowledging mistakes and holding convictions.

Rather than a dismissal or a defense, I would like to initiate a discussion.

This is not intended to be an all-encompassing explanation—it is the beginning of a discussion. It is a spark. And the discussion is important, because I believe that the negative perceptions about Christianity are actually misconceptions. I believe Jesus was a master of tolerance. I believe a rational person can worship an invisible God. And I believe Jesus is not only relevant to our lives, but that without him there is no life at all.

But I also believe that these misconceptions have formed because Christians (I am including myself in this) have misrepresented Jesus. The church has, at times, been intolerant, irrational, and terribly irrelevant. So the discussion needs to involve both confession and clarification. We need to own our mistakes and then move toward clarifying the misconceptions of Christianity.

I am seeking to own my part in this and also to bring clarity. I want to set some records straight and right some wrongs. I want to give a fair picture of what this movement is supposed to be about. And then we will each be left to choose how to respond.

There have always been varied reactions to this Jesus and the religion that formed in his wake. There have been those who loudly reject, those who quietly abstain, those who admire from a distance, and then a few who decide to follow. However each of us responds to Christianity, my hope is that we can make that decision based on good information. Often I think people are reacting to a distorted version of this religion. If we are going to walk away from Christianity, we should at least know what we are actually walking away from.

And there is a chance that once we realize what we were walking away from, we may decide to turn around.

PART I: INTOLERANT

"One day she asked my friend, 'Don't you want to go to heaven?' In a weary exasperation he responded, 'Not if it's full of people like you.'"

—a story told by Martin Thielen

PART I: INTOLERANT

There is a popular bumper sticker these days. I've seen it parked on the street covered in ice crystals, idling at a stoplight behind a wall of smoke, or driving down the interstate toward Chicago. It says one simple word: coexist. A series of various religious symbols form the letters (the "t" is a Christian cross, for example). There are different ways one could interpret the sticker. But I think the goal is to give a visual representation of an abstract concept we call tolerance.

It is a simple picture, all these religions standing next to each other. They are each clearly distinct, and yet they remain in close proximity to one another. And I think this is what is meant by tolerance. It begins with the premise that there are actually different ideas—all religions do not say the same thing. And then it moves to suggest that people of different religions can live in the same apartment building, learn in the same schools, and get gas at the same pump—all without killing each other. They can coexist. And even more, the can demonstrate acts of love toward one another.

Unfortunately, this is not what usually happens. What usually happens is that people pick one half or the other. Some agree that there are undeniable differences between religions. But they would suggest these differences mean we should not stand together. They suggest instead we should segregate. We should divide. And if needed, we should take up a fight against the various parties who disagree with us. This is actually called intolerance.

Then there are those who believe passionately that we should stand together. But they believe this on the basis there really are no differences at all between religions. All nuances and variations dissolve. All religions say the same thing, so we should pursue peace. This seems closer to tolerance, but it is actually something else. Tolerance is only possible if ideas are actually different. (Why else would you need to tolerate someone?) The belief that says there are no differences is called relativism.

Christianity is not intolerant. However, many Christians are. And oftentimes, this intolerance leads people to recoil and retreat into relativism. All of this is very odd because it could be argued that Jesus is the most tolerant person who ever lived. So where did we go wrong? And for that matter, where do we go from here?

CHAPTER 1

SHOES LACED WITH EXPLOSIVES

Some Christians are intolerant.

Religion is core to a person's identity. This is true of Christianity as much as any other religion. If our religion feels challenged or threatened, it can evoke fear, and fear can bring us to lash out. Though Christianity is not a religion that teaches intolerance, Christians have often fallen to fear and come to see other religions and worldviews as a threat. Consequently, they have interacted with the world in a way that does not represent the model of Jesus.

For many years, I harbored intolerance toward Muslims. My understanding of Islam consisted of a series of images: black smoke lifting from metal buildings, an old man with a wiry beard wearing a head wrap and a camouflage jacket, and a parade of Arab men filling the street, lifting automatic weapons in the air like beer mugs after the world cup. To me, this was Islam. It was the religion that sowed violence and messed up airports.

I remember when the media first started reporting on heightened airport security. Various travelers were being subjected to full-body scanning. They passed through machines that rendered them naked on a screen—virtual, public strip searches. Privacy was eliminated and, with it, a portion of human dignity. It wasn't just the planes hijacked one fall morning. There were others smuggling explosives onto airplanes. I once read about creative ways people were trying to blow things up. One method involved placing plastic explosives in the sole of a shoe.

And the result was that I wanted to be distant from Muslim people and their shoes.

I was not outwardly intolerant; it was a matter of the heart. But then a shift surprised me. I read a book written by a Muslim man. I talked to a Muslim woman. And I met a kid who spent a long time in Morocco and left with the sense that the Muslims he'd lived among were the kindest people he'd ever met. My intolerance started to dissolve.

I still believe there are undeniable differences between my system of beliefs and the teachings of Islam. I believe terrorism is real and that certain branches of Islam endorse this violence. But I also believe there are many Muslims who do not stand in alignment with these zealous members of their religion. I saw people discussing a proposition to build a mosque near the property where the World Trade Center used to stand. There was an interview with a Muslim woman in favor of the mosque. She made a simple but important point. Though the buildings were destroyed by Muslims steering a plane, the buildings were also occupied by Muslims working that day. Some of the families that lost loved ones were Muslim families.

All this is to say it is possible for a Christian to stand next to a Muslim in mutual respect and friendship. While I am learning to retrain my mind, I recognize I am not the only Christian who has drifted toward intolerance.

I was once driving down the street and passed a small church building. There was a welcome sign in front of the church near the street. It had a message board with removable letters, like at a gas station. Most churches will list their service times or offer encouragement to those driving by. This welcome sign contained a message of condemnation toward homosexuals. Really—it was on the welcome sign.

There are the black-and-white images I can recall from somewhere, probably a book, of passionate and pasty people holding up signs with the simple and ignorant words "God Is White."

A small crowd of people from a church in Kansas made a trip up to Indiana to picket the church we used to attend. The pastor and some of his family members accused the leaders of our church of preaching lies. So they paced along the sidewalk in front of our building holding two or three signs each. The first sign that came into view said "God Hates You."

In recent years, one pastor rose up as the icon of Christian intolerance. This Florida-based holy man had short white hair and a handgun at his waist. Other than among the fifty-some people who faithfully attended his church, he was basically unknown. But when he tossed out the suggestion Christians should take part in a book burning to commemorate 9/11, he landed himself into the public eye and into the scope of every major government entity involved with homeland security.[1] "Burn a Koran Day" never got fully off the ground. Whether it was pressure from the government or just common sense grabbing him by the throat and slapping him awake, the militant pastor never carried out his plan. But his intent was unmistakably clear.

Others have taken their intolerance further. I read about another man who is currently serving multiple life sentences in prison. In addition to building and detonating a bomb at the Olympic Games, he decided it would be a good idea to blow up an abortion clinic. His decision took one life and maimed another. In his trial, the bomber said, "Abortion is murder, and because it is murder I believe deadly force is needed to stop it."[2] Some may question whether he was acting out of some distorted Christian convictions or whether he was just acting out of pure distortion. But his rhetoric involved traces of Biblical references, and his life is spotted with traces of destruction.

More distant history is saturated with examples of intolerance from people marching under a Christian flag. A whole book (or several of them) would be required to touch the Crusades or the Inquisition where Christians were not only killing followers of other religions, but also killing each other. It would be futile to attempt a brief summary in these pages. The issues are too complex and the evil too vast.

The question in response to all of this is Why? Why have so many Christians displayed such an extensive intolerance? The answer is many of us believe the plane is going to crash. Let me explain what I mean.

Life is like flying on an airplane. It begins quietly. The world is a rubber room so small the soft walls literally hold us in place. Then we leave the womb and the world begins to grow. This first transition is somewhat drastic, like when a plane first leaves the ground. We leave the dark and warm and safe to join the bright and cold and unknown. And we squint our eyes, suck in air, and scream to heaven. From this point, it is a simple reality that our world will continue to change.

If the changes are gradual, we are not likely to even notice or remember them, just as the ascent of a plane is usual uneventful. Chew a stick of gum and you will hardly notice your body climbing thirty thousand feet in the air. In many cultures, newborn babies are carried close to the mother in some sort of wrap or pouch. The rhythm of the same beating heart vibrates against the body of a baby strapped to her mother. Eventually the world includes a crib and then a bed, a single room becomes a house, and a house becomes a village or neighborhood.

People get added to our worlds as well. The human population expands to include not only our parents and siblings but also the neighbor kid who steals our bicycle and the lady at the grocery store and the man who drives past the house in a garbage truck once a week. Depending on where you live, your world may begin to include people who actually look different from you.

The world subtly gets bigger—and by that I mean our perception of the world. More information gets added, and so our understanding of reality has to adjust accordingly. Most of us don't get too worked up over these small adjustments.

But what happens when the changes to our worlds are not subtle? What happens when change comes violently? Parents divorce, a sibling dies, a home burns, a war breaks out—these changes can ravage us. I heard on the news about a woman who'd written a book about her husband. They'd been happily married for years and even had small children when she learned he was a pedophile. This turbulence is a problem. When the aircraft begins to lurch and shake to the point that the drink cart dumps cranberry juice in your lap or suitcases start falling out of the overhead compartments, we become fearful. The world becomes unsafe, and we want to steady it and regain control.

We all react differently to these turbulent changes in life—these things that shake up our version of the world. Some of us turn inward. We check our seatbelts and pray. Others of us take aggressive action in an attempt to regain a sense of order. We pull down oxygen masks and inflate life jackets. We yell at the stewardess or storm the cockpit to take over the controls. What does any of this have to do with religion?

Our religion and our morality are core to our identities. They run as deep as our bones. These fundamental beliefs often come from our families and are absorbed early. We begin to pick up ideas about God from our parents and our communities. A picture of God slowly comes into view. The image becomes sharper over time. We get an image of God that we hold onto. For those who inherited the belief that there is no God, the picture shows an empty room. Regardless of what the picture looks like, our understanding of God is a major component of our reality—of our normal. When someone comes along and starts to suggest that our picture is incomplete or starts to erase part of the picture and draw in something else, we can begin to panic.

For a long time I thought everyone was Lutheran, except for the Catholics. Eventually I discovered that religious views include everything thing from atheism to Islam. They include the millions of Hindu gods and the absence of a god within Buddhism. And all these ideas about God started to make me uneasy. I felt my control slipping away as I saw all of these people altering my picture of God and therefore challenging my foundational beliefs.

I was never directly under attack from anyone. No one was burning down churches or refusing to shop at my store because I was a Christian. I never even felt a verbal threat. The feeling of attack came from the fact that these people saw the world differently. And it messed with my safe and clean view of God. It felt like the plane was beginning to shake apart.

Our picture of God can only get so big before we need to bring it back in. We need to regain control and remove the threats to restore things to our normal. And so many of us put up walls to keep out those things that challenge our religion. This is where intolerance is born. Often it is a quiet intolerance or indifference. This was me—I just pretended these others views didn't exist, or I held oversimplified definitions of other religions so they would be easy to dismiss. Others will go to greater lengths to insulate their religious views—not just retreating, but seeking to silence or remove the opposition as well. I believe this is why we see the violent actions from Christians I described previously. And this religious intolerance is not actually limited to Christianity.

I already alluded to the violence that feels common in extreme Islam. Similarly, there are Hindu extremist groups ushering in waves of violence in Nepal. An article found on the Voice of the Martyrs website reported that one group issued a standing threat to bomb the homes of any Christians who refused to stop spreading the gospel.[3]

Then there is the Israeli-Palestinian conflict. The Jewish state of Israel has often been a target, but it has also instigated violence in the current conflicts with Palestine. This conflict is a religious one. In his book *Son of Hamas*, Mosab Hassan Yousef described his encounter with Israeli police. Mosab was a Muslim. He was arrested and later shared the experience.

> As I tried to contort my body so that it would fit into the small area usually reserved for people's feet, one beefy soldier put his boot squarely on my hip and pressed the muzzle of his M16 assault rifle into my chest. The hot reek of petrol fumes saturated the floor of the vehicle and forced my throat closed. Whenever I tried to adjust my cramped position, the solider jabbed the gun barrel deeper into my chest. Without warning, a searing pain shot through my body and made my toes clench. It was as if a rocket were exploding in my skull.[4]

Violent intolerance can even be seen from those opposed to religion in general. Consider the Soviet regime. Author Benjamin Wiker described the terror of Lenin and Stalin well when he used the phrase "unimaginable butchery." The former oversaw the killing of six to eight million people, and the latter saw perhaps four times that amount.[5] In these cases, those who did not adhere to the Communist dogma posed a threat and were therefore removed.

One could argue that there are other motives besides fear tied into all this violence. Perhaps someone blows up an abortion clinic or destroys a tower because that person believes it is the right thing to do, as though it is a moral obligation. And perhaps the Soviet leaders killed their people because they wanted power and nothing more. But I would argue that even in these cases, the extremist is killing because there is a perceived threat. And this means fear is present—which is the point. Intolerance is the result of fear and self-preservation. Those who are different or disagree with our ideals pose a danger to us, and we seek to avoid or remove that danger. Like wounded animals, we lash out.

Years ago I was standing in my garage with the neighbor kid, and we were arguing. I was very upset with him for something, mainly because I couldn't convince him to agree with me. So what did I do to resolve the issue?

I bit him. Seriously. I bit the neighbor kid, right on the arm. I actually drew blood. I am going to assume that he also probably remembers this event—not what we were arguing about, but what it felt like to receive a serious flesh wound. When people get bitten they tend to recoil and pull back. If you get bitten enough, you may retreat altogether to a place where there are no open mouths with teeth.

See, there is fallout from all of this intolerance. After hearing all of the arguments and watching the separation and possibly even getting bitten on the arm, many people have decided to just leave. They have decided the whole thing is a joke and that it would be better to just get off this plane because it is crashing anyway. So they kick open the emergency door and taste the wind pouring out from under the wing. They strap on a chute, lean forward, and allow the fierce air to wrap around their bodies as the ground pulls them through space toward everything and nothing all at once.

This free-falling, wide-open place that so many have jumped into is called relativism. It is the idea that all religions are really the same and that truth is subjective. There are no differences and therefore no reasons to fight. It can seem like a valid response to all of the trials caused by religious fighting. And it warrants some further discussion.

CHAPTER 2

WEATHERMAN

Many have turned to relativism thinking it is the same as tolerance.
Relativism says all ideas are true, or no ideas are true. The individual can determine truth and the implication is that all religions can carry on at peace with each other because all competition for truth has been eliminated. The problem with relativism is that it does not align with the reality of our experiences.

To fully surrender to the claims of relativism, we would have to concede that all truth is subjective and therefore nothing is absolutely true. And most people wouldn't go that far. We are still okay with some things being absolutely true. I am six feet two inches tall. I grew up in a town called Ham Lake. These things are just factual statements. They can all be easily verified. These facts about me could also be referred to as truths. There are plenty of things out there like this that are just true. Not too many people sit around arguing about who won (or lost) the 2004 World Series. These topics are easy. Discussions about your hometown or your painful dedication to a losing team are not threatening. But what happens when this discussion of truth turns to more serious matters?

Talk about morality or the existence of God and we become weary of claims to truth. Talk about religion and we don't want to hear it. Why? We've seen the carnage from religious zealots. At this point we decide we would rather live in a relativistic world where there is no absolute anything. This is where the prospect of skydiving becomes appealing and we step over the edge.

We are more comfortable out in the breezy middle where our cheeks can flap in the wind. We prefer to take a very loose approach to religion. Anything goes. All religions say basically the same thing. Praying to Allah is no different than praying to Jehovah, which is no different than praying to a potted plant.

Author Martha Sherrill captured the spirit of the age when she wrote, "So we're browsing the spiritual marketplace, dropping new ideas and philosophies into our carts—a smidgen of Buddhism, some New Testament, maybe a little Tai chi tossed in."[1] Nobody fights in this type of environment. We are all just pushing carts through the grocery store, letting others with less in their carts cut in front of us in line. This is very appealing, and I believe it is motivated by a genuine desire for peace (as well as a fear of being labeled intolerant). The problem is that it doesn't actually work in reality.

Ravi Zacharias told a story of an experience in which he observed a mob of people worshiping a golden statue. He asked a woman if the god represented by the statue actually existed. She responded, "If you think in your heart that he exists, then he does."

Ravi probed further and asked, "What if you believe he does not exist?"

"Then he doesn't exist," the woman responded.[2]

That strikes me as an odd perspective—a chunk of gold becoming a real functioning deity simply because someone believes in it? If there is no God, I cannot conjure him into existence by closing my eyes and just believing really hard. And if there is a God, I cannot cause him to vaporize by choosing to deny his existence. That would be like a fly grabbing the swatter out of a man's hand and slapping him on the forehead. Furthermore, if God actually exists, this deity would have specific characteristics that are beyond my influence.

When it comes to God, we want to fall back into relativism. But I've come to realize there is no such thing as selective relativism. We can't say truth applies to baseball but not religion. It is all or nothing. If you want to subscribe to relativism, it must be an absolute relativism. So what would that look like?

It threatened to snow on our wedding day. My wife and I got married at the end of April, in Fargo, North Dakota. It snows a lot in Fargo. Actually, it snows a fair amount, and then the wind blows fiercely, lifting the fallen snow into the air and whipping it around so it feels like it is always snowing. The snow drifts like giant sand dunes because there is no protection from the wind. Trees are scarce and the land is flat and wide. Combines drive side by side like an offensive line, chewing through the cornfields.

I didn't want it to snow on our wedding day. My wife gets cold easily. Even if she were blue she would be beautiful, but I wanted her to feel comfortable in a wedding dress. We have only one or two pictures of us outside because it was so cold that day. Even though I did not want the snow and cold, I couldn't stop it because I can't control the weather.

There was a movie made a while back called *Bruce Almighty*. It starred Jim Carrey, who played a weatherman. The basic idea was that this guy was endowed with supernatural powers. Among these powers, he gains the ability to control the weather. The problem is, he is driven by selfishness and he abuses his power. In the end, Jim Carrey goes back to being a regular weatherman, and he is much happier.

Can you imagine us all having the power to control the weather? Utter chaos. Or what if we all had the power to do whatever we wanted? What if we were all running around speaking things into existence or destroying things that annoyed us? The universe would deteriorate very quickly.

If we did live in a universe where each person could create his or her own reality, we would experience absolute relativism. There would be no standard or steadiness, because the universe would be in constant flux—leaping to the will of a billion tiny gods. Everything would be true and nothing would be true.

But we don't live in a universe like this. We all have a will and we have the ability to make choices that impact reality and influence other people. And we often exercise our will in selfish ways. But none of us have unlimited power to supplement our will. We can't change reality or create our own realities. We are all grounded to a reality that is beyond us. Things happen all over the world every day that none of us have control over. Truth exists independently of us. Some of these truths are just less accessible than others.

Normally, if my wife asks me the temperature in the house, I just walk over to the thermostat and say, "It is sixty-eight degrees." Assuming the thermostat is not broken, it is safe to conclude I've given her a truthful answer. Shortly after we moved into our house, the thermostat broke. If my wife had asked me the temperature at that point, the answer would not have been accessible to me. There was still an actual temperature in the room; I just didn't have a way to verify it. So we called the home warranty company, who sent out a kid to fix the problem. He shocked himself three or four times in the process of inspecting wires in our furnace and ended up replacing the thermostat. Because he had surrendered his hand to the flames, I could again verify the true temperature in my home.

There are certain truths we are removed from—instances when the proverbial thermostat is broken. If the gap in space or time increases, it becomes more difficult to verify truth.

There are people who think the moon landing was staged. I've never been to the moon. I am removed from this event; I have to make a judgment call. I have to look at the evidence and decide whether I believe it is true. I may have to trust the input of other people. But regardless of what I believe, if Neil Armstrong actually walked on the moon, there is nothing that can erase that fact.

There are also those who deny the Holocaust. Though I didn't bear witness to the horror, I could travel to Europe and see the graves. I could walk through a concentration camp and stand under rusted showerheads that once poured down gas. I could talk to an old man in a nursing home who was dragged through that hellish gutter and survived. The individual who denies perhaps the most massive crime against humanity cannot undo reality. It happened.

Conspiracy theories surface during discussions of historical events because we are removed from these events. Our access to the truth is limited. But the truth still exists out there, whether or not we can reach it. It stands waiting for someone to retrieve it—just like a lonely American flag pinned to the surface of the moon.

If measurable space and time separate us from these worldly events, how great is the distance that separates us from God? To say the gaps are bigger is a gross understatement. But even so, this does not exclude absolute truth from the conversation.

God either exists or doesn't exist. One of those statements is true. Certainly it is difficult to arrive at the answer. Here the truth hangs further out on the tree. We will have to slide out until the branch bends and threatens to snap in order to reach it. But the truth is there. It is a reality independent of us.

Relativism does not work as an answer to intolerance because it does not work as an answer to anything. Even so, it seems like a less destructive option. We choose it because it seems like the peaceful path. It feels like tolerance. But it is not.

Real tolerance is far more difficult. To practice true tolerance, we can't just pretend to erase differences. The differences are there. And to be a person of tolerance means to love in spite of those differences. It means loving even our perceived enemies.

CHAPTER 3

YOU'LL PUT YOUR EYE OUT

Christianity is a tolerant religion.

This may sound like an odd statement based on the behavior of many Christians. But representatives can misrepresent. Students can sometimes neglect the instruction of their teacher. So what did Jesus teach? He once told his friend to put away his sword during a struggle with his enemy. But he also said he came to bring a sword and that his teaching would divide people. He did not condone violent intolerance but neither did he teach relativism. Jesus taught something far more difficult. He taught love for the enemy.[1] This is true tolerance. Jesus was unwavering in his convictions, and therefore some counted him an enemy. Yet he demonstrated unprecedented love for those enemies. Then he implored his followers to do the same. In order to understand this, we must first clarify what an enemy is. Then we can consider what it looks like to love one.

What do you think of when you hear the word enemy? I was robbed once. A kid stole a pencil drawing I did in art class. It had taken me weeks to finish. Then, one day, he lifted the drawing, leaving an empty frame on the wall. I can still see the blank wall through the glass of the frame. A few years before that, the house across the street from us was burglarized. As my parents talked about it, I thought of a man in black clothes, like a ninja, climbing down the stucco walls and disappearing past the street light with a TV balanced on his back. And in the city where I grew up, my family knew of a man who lost his wife because she surprised the felons who broke into their house. I imagined a gunshot and then a laundry basket spilling down the stairs.

The thief and the murderer are easy to identify as enemies. Jesus addressed both of them when he was teaching about loving enemies. He said that if someone takes your coat, you should give him your cloak as well. And if someone strikes you on the right cheek, you should offer the other.² Then he demonstrated what this looked like. Below his feet, the men who had just crucified him were gambling over his clothes. And as he died, Jesus prayed for their forgiveness.³ This type of a response is almost unthinkable.

But an enemy is not just the one who threatens my property or my life. As we have been discussing, the one who threatens my religion could also be seen as an enemy.

Jesus was a Jew. The religion of Judaism has known many enemies. During Jesus' lifetime one of the primary religious conflicts existed between Jews and Samaritans. The two groups claimed common ancestry, both descendants of Abraham. But early in their history the kingdom split. As the people divided, their religion divided with them. People inclined to worship often designate a specific place to carry out devotion to the object of that worship. For Jews, that place was a temple built on a hill in Jerusalem. The Samaritans also built a temple. Their temple sat on Mount Gerizim.⁴ In the end, there were two groups climbing different mountains, both trying to reach the same God. Each group rejected the other's attempts at worship and deemed the other a religious enemy.

A story is told about Jesus talking to a woman from Samaria. They were sitting by a well, and the woman said to Jesus, "Our fathers worshiped on this mountain, but you Jews claim that the place where we must worship is in Jerusalem." Jesus acknowledged the differences between Samaritans and Jews, validating the woman's observation. But then he went on to say that both groups had actually misunderstood the meaning of true worship. He asserted that people didn't need to go to a mountain to find God. They needed to go to God himself.⁵

Jesus didn't try to dissolve the religious differences between Samaritans and Jews. He didn't say all paths led to God. He said they were both wrong and then he introduced a new path altogether. What is fascinating about Jesus is the way he talked about Samaritans despite the chasm that existed.

Jesus told a story about a Jewish man assaulted and left by the road to die. Two Jewish religious leaders avoided the broken man, a member of their own religion, and kept walking. The one who finally stopped and saved the man was a Samaritan.[6] His religious "enemy" was assigned the role of hero in his story—Jesus was esteeming this man.

He seemed to be suggesting a radical love between religious enemies. Then he demonstrated what that looks like. Jesus once passed a group of men with leprosy (most likely some form of dramatic skin disease, not to be confused the more modern disease, which attacks the nervous system). This sickness rendered people unclean and barred them from their communities and even their religions. They were the dirty ones. There were ten men in all—nine Jews and one Samaritan. Jesus stopped at their request for pity. He told all of them, including the Samaritan, to go to the priests. On the way, Jesus removed the disease of every man—one of whom was his religious "enemy." This act of love must have stirred the Samaritan, because he was the only one who showed gratitude. He returned to Jesus and fell with his face in the dirt.[7]

Religion still has the power to create enemies just as it did during Jesus' life. In the book *Son of Hamas* mentioned earlier, Mosab Hassan Yousef spoke extensively about the Palestinian conflict. Both Israeli Jews and Palestinian Muslims are suffering as violence entangles them, as though that region is wrapped in barbed wire. Among other things, they too are fighting over rights to worship on a particular hill in Jerusalem. The Jewish temple once stood there, and now a mosque stands above its ruins.

Mosab's book is filled with imagery of this conflict. He described how the cemetery in his neighborhood was their soccer field—a cemetery that was crowded with corpses, with more added every day. Jewish people were stoned in the street, and Israeli citizens driving in armored cars and carrying automatic weapons were shooting Palestinians. He recalled how "the water storage tanks on our roof were shredded by Israeli bullets."[8]

Mosab grew up always trying to identify who his enemies were. Then someone told him that Jesus taught people to love their enemies. It was this concept that shook him loose and eventually led him to a lake one night, where a friend baptized him in secret.[9] He began to act as an ambassador of peace. He offered intelligence to Israeli officials and protection to his Muslim father—all in an attempt to dismantle the conflicts and disrupt terrorism. He came to count as friends many of the people he once hated. He came to be a breathing example of the worshiper Jesus described to the Samaritan woman at the well. True worshipers will not worship God on a mountain; they will worship in spirit and in truth. They will not need to climb up to a temple, because they will become temples—the dwelling place of God.

While I believe Mosab's story is impactful, it may seem distant or obscure for some. The religious conflicts that feel more common to many of us don't involve issues of worship or religious tradition. They involve issues of morality.

Jesus was a firm moral teacher. One of the moral issues Jesus preached about extensively was the issue adultery. In Matthew's gospel Jesus explained that the sexual bond formed between a husband and wife cannot be severed. As a result, he asserted that if anyone divorced his spouse, other than for reasons of infidelity, he would cause her to commit adultery if she ever remarried.[10]

He also taught that if a man looks upon a woman and lusts for her, he is an adulterer. At the level of this man's heart, he has already committed an affair, even though he never touched the woman. Jesus emphasized this teaching so fiercely that he suggested it would be better for a man to put out his own eye then to fall to lust—better to be blind than to be impure.[11]

This is an absolute sense of morality. Jesus issued a firm moral standard and suggested that it applies to everyone. For some, his teaching seems simply impossible. For others, these words have power to stir resentment. We may be quick to deem him judgmental, archaic, and even unfair. And yet he managed to carry the balance of fierce conviction and fierce love. He blasted the act of adultery but showed dangerous kindness to those guilty of it.

In one instance, Jesus was in the temple courts, where people had surrounded him to hear him teach. As he was sitting down to speak, the Pharisees hauled a woman before him. They proceeded to humiliate the woman by publicly condemning her for engaging in adulterous acts. And based on their words, it seems they were intent on executing her for her crimes. Jesus suggested that the one among them who was sinless should be the first to beat her with a stone. At this, each accuser left until all were gone. Not only did Jesus withhold condemnation from this woman, but he also saved her life.[12]

He encountered others carrying the same type of damage inflicted by an adulterous life style. This included the Samaritan woman discussed earlier. In every case Jesus offered redemption. So although he displayed no tolerance for what he considered to be immoral acts, he also proved to be the manifestation of perfect tolerance toward the souls who came to him in search of life.

Disagreements on moral issues seem to be some of the fiercest battles, and when Christians are branded as intolerant, it is almost always tied to morality. While so many Christians have dispensed intolerance over these types of issues, there are some who understand the model Jesus laid out.

I once attended a Christian conference as a high school student. I was listening to a woman speak on the issue of abortion from a Christian perspective. She was opposed to abortion under any circumstance. This is what most would expect from a Christian. Most people would also expect to absorb a spirit of judgment from this type of person. But this woman was not yelling at people from a stage. She had a reason for her moral stance, but it was different than you might think.

The speaker shared a very fragile and difficult story. She told of a woman who had been raped. The condemnable crime led to a pregnancy. Though most would understand and support the decision to end things, the woman did not abort the baby. She carried the child, gave birth, and then placed the little girl up for adoption. As the woman spoke, the room was frozen. The end of her story revealed the source of her deep convictions. The rape victim was her mother. The room melted, leaving puddles on the carpet of the hotel conference room.

She did not spend her life spreading condemnation for those who had chosen abortion. She spent her life offering grace to those who had suffered through it and hope for those who were considering it. She didn't bring judgment; she brought a chance at redemption.

Jesus demonstrated radical tolerance. No one had ever taught people to love their enemies. He proved tolerance is possible. This was nothing less than a revolution. And some have joined the revolution, engaging in ridiculous acts of love toward enemies. But this type of tolerance is still rare. The question is—why?

If someone set off a car bomb in front of a restaurant where I was eating I would be infuriated at the injustice and evil of such an action. But the reality is, I've felt angry when a person cuts in front of me in line at a restaurant. I get upset with the person who questions my honesty. And I become intolerant toward the person who challenges my religion (knowingly or unknowingly). It doesn't take much for me to deem someone an enemy. C. S. Lewis said, "Everyone feels benevolent if nothing happens to be annoying him at the moment."[13]

The reason tolerance is rare is because loving one's enemies is extremely difficult in practice. Everything in us screams against it. It feels much easier to identify our enemies and hate them. Jesus may have lived differently, along with a small number of followers, but most don't.

The reality is, when people hold strong convictions about God or religion, it almost always ends in fighting. And so we come to question whether there is any point in holding religious convictions. Why risk it? Why not just let go of religion and let it float off into space like a balloon released from the hand of a child? Then we could go on with our lives in peace. We don't have to accept relativism. It is okay to concede that truth exists. We just need to recognize it is beyond our reach.

There are many who believe this. The common term for this view is agnosticism. Simply put, truth is real, but it is inaccessible. Maybe even God is real, but we could never know for sure if he exists, and we certainly could not come to know him personally. If this is true, then there is probably not any point in pursuing religion. Because generally, when someone takes a religious path, he or she is taking that road with the hope of finding God—with the hope that it will lead somewhere.

But what if agnosticism is misguided? What if it is actually possible to reach up and grab onto truth? What if it is possible to come to know God? If that is the case, I should think the pursuit of this God could be worth everything we have.

CHAPTER 4

THE INVISIBLE ELEPHANT

It is possible to know God.

If someone willingly reveals him or herself, it is possible to know that person. Without revelation, there can be no knowing. Coming to know a person is one thing. But coming to know God is something completely different. The first question is whether or not God exists. And if God exists, we need to know if he has chosen to reveal himself.

There is a process involved in getting to know someone. The act of knowing begins in the mind. Our minds are like a gutter. By gutter, I mean a long aluminum trough that outlines the roof of a house. The rain falls on the roof, rolls down the shingles, and collects in the gutter. The water then swells and flows toward the end, where it travels down like a waterfall in a tunnel. Eventually, the water spills onto the ground.

Our minds collect all the information that rains down on us. That information eventually lands on the soil of the heart. By heart, I don't mean the chambered machine planted in our chests. I am referring to the soul. Call it what you like. It is one of those things that are difficult to label and yet we all know are real. It is the place in us that sometimes feels at war with our minds. This is the place we actually make important decisions and believe or disbelieve things. This is where love and hate and passion and apathy dwell. So information and experiences come to us through our senses. We go around seeing and hearing and touching and tasting and smelling. We process this in our minds, and then it moves to our hearts and shapes who we are and what we actually believe.

This is how we come to know people. First we take in information—just some basic facts. When I first saw Heather, I noticed her eyes. They always watered at the corners when she laughed, almost to the point where she couldn't keep them open. I also noticed an elegant tattoo on her neck that could only be seen when she wore her hair up. After speaking with her I learned she was studying social work, and I sensed a deep authenticity in her character.

In some cases, this is as far as we go. We just know a few things about a person. At this surface level, not much actually falls down into the heart. But then there are some people we don't just know about, but whom we actually know. Heather went from being the beautiful social worker with an intriguing tattoo to being my wife, the one I know on the deepest possible human level.

I never knew my mom's dad. He died when she was young. I know he existed, or else I wouldn't be here. And I know things about him. I've heard stories and seen yellowed photographs. He was a shorter man but strong. He smoked cigars and he worked hard. He was a teacher for a while. His students ranged in age from five to forty-five and included a German man who didn't speak English. After that he sold cars and owned real estate. He didn't believe in carrying debt and paid for his house in cash. My mom tells stories of how he used to take them to the hardware store and find coins in his pocket so they could buy candy.

Though I know about my grandfather, I didn't know him personally. I would have liked to. I really would have liked to know that man. It is my knowledge of him through my mom's stories that compels me to want to know him. But for now we are separated by time.

Then there is Heather's grandpa. I also collected stories about him. Heather told me when they were little they'd sit at her grandparents' table for a meal and her grandpa always in the same seat. If they looked away or got distracted, he would steal their cookies or dump some more peas on their plates, always with a steady face, like an old card player. He prayed before every meal and always thanked his wife for the food when leaving the table.

He used to hang gum in a tree behind their house. They thought it was a gum tree. And he would make a skating rink for the neighborhood kids in the winter. When he got older, he'd sit in his recliner next to a potted cactus and watch through the large windows at the corner of the living room as the school bus made its route.

But in addition to Heather's stories, I also had conversations and interactions with him. I knew him personally for a few years before he died. By the time I came to know him, he was an older man. But he would always shake my hand firmly and smile when I'd see him. He'd ask where we lived again and want to know how long my dad had worked for the railroad. He'd talk about how he worked for the highway department and how he was once a drinker and a fighter but gave up alcohol as a very young man. Then he'd look up and tell me to stay away from the drink. Sometimes, he'd talk about the war with his large hand on his forehead. He'd get really quiet when he talked about the war.

He also wrote things down—events and such. The walls of the shed behind their house were filled with writing. He'd even written a date under the bill of his hat. It was a way of remembering, I think—important things, like when Kennedy was shot and his wedding anniversary.

So we begin with knowing about someone and move into a personal knowing, from some facts splattered in our minds to an intimacy at the level of the heart. The only way we can actually know someone is to interact with that person. And at some level, that individual must be willing to reveal themselves to us. The degree to which I know someone depends on their proximity and the amount of information they willingly reveal. If this is true of people, I think it would also apply to knowing God.

Is it possible to know God? This is God we are talking about. If God exists, he is other, different, huge; he is supernatural and we are natural. Maybe God exists and there are things that are true about him. But how could we ever know these things? We can't even see God. How could we possibly know him? These are valid questions.

This discussion is a common one, and it often turns to elephants. I first came across the story while reading the book *The Reason for God* by Timothy Keller.[1] It is found in other places as well. It goes something like this.

There are these three men who are blind. They run into this elephant, who sits very still as they examine him. They don't know that it is an elephant because they are blind. Relying on their sense of touch, the three men begin to argue about the being they've just discovered. The first man finds this being to be long and slinky like a snake. He has, of course, grabbed onto the elephant's trunk. The second man believes that he has found a tree. The piece of elephant he is touching is thick and round—the elephant's leg. And the third man has come to yet another conclusion. This being, whatever it may be, is large and flat. This man was touching the side of the creature. Why the elephant did not stampede the three men prodding at him, I am not sure, but that is not the point, of course.

The idea is that we are all blind. None of us can see God or really know God, so the best we can do is argue about him. But Keller points out a flaw that is very easy to miss in this story. There is one participant who isn't blind. It's the narrator. The one telling the story is standing back and can see the whole thing. It is as though the narrator has been given eyes to see the elephant for what it really is.

Maybe that is what we need—eyes to see God. If we could get eyes to see, then we could know God. But this gets messy and actually even dangerous. There are all kinds of people walking around claiming they've been given eyes to see—each claiming he or she possesses better eyes than everyone else. Even within one religion there can be groups that claim to see God more clearly. This happens all the time in Christianity.

How can one person claim to have better eyesight than another? Who is seeing God, and who is seeing what they want to see? It seems like this just lands us back in blind arguments—steering again toward intolerance. Unless it is not about our eyesight at all.

This is actually not about us learning to see or some seeing better than others. The suggestion from Christianity is not that we climbed the mountain to see God, but that God decided to make himself visible to us. The claim is that God came into close proximity and revealed himself in a way everyone could see.

I am thinking about the elephant. If the elephant had just said, "Hey, I'm an elephant—now leave me alone," this would have cleared things up for the poor men arguing about snakes and trees and large, flat things. I realize elephants can't speak, but I believe God can.

Our kids love to play hide-and-seek with Heather and me. There are only about three hiding places in our house they can access: behind the curtains, behind the couch, or in a closet. If a sleeping bag happens to be lying around, they will crawl under it and become a pile of blankets.

Heather and I hide in the same places the kids do. And I'm not a small man, so it is difficult to conceal myself. But even though they find me within seconds, there is always a spurt of laughter, as if they were completely caught off guard. We love for them to find us.

But I do have access to other hiding places—places the kids cannot go. If I wanted, I could run out the garage, climb up onto the roof, and sit there like a pigeon, and they would never find me. Even if they made it outside the house, the roof is too high. Their perspective would prevent them from even being capable of looking on the roof. We reveal ourselves, or at least leave noticeable signs, because we want them to find us.

If God exists, he could choose to sit perched on a rooftop, hiding from us. Or he could choose to reveal himself to us. And if God has willingly provided this revelation, then it would be possible to know things about him—or better yet, to start to know him personally. So we could know not just whether God has a tattoo, but also what his emotions are and what he cares about and what he thinks about us. I've been told by some it is trite to compare God to a father playing with his children. They may be right—unless God actually is a father. In that case it would not be trite at all.

I am not saying I believe we can know everything about God. There are major regions of my wife's heart that are a beautiful mystery to me, and we eat from the same bowl of cereal some mornings. I am coming to know her more but not yet fully. Amplify this a million times with God. But the point is, there is progress toward an actual relationship—a real knowing.

If God exists and has revealed himself to the world as the Christian claims, we should expect to see movement behind a curtain and lumps under a blanket. We should expect to see traces of the divine mixed in with the normal. We should expect to look out at this vast universe and at least hear the echo of God.

PART II: IRRATIONAL

You believe that the Bible is the most profound book ever written and that its contents have stood the test of time …
All of these beliefs are false.

—Sam Harris

PART II: IRRATIONAL

We used to bring our old hot dog buns down to this pond to feed the fish. I sometimes wonder what the fish thought about this. What were they thinking as they heard a plopping sound followed by soft waves washing over their gills? How would the fish understand this meal? The foreign food came from somewhere. I like to think the fish talked about theology in these moments.

The Old Testament includes a story similar to that of the drainage pond. The Israelites were dwelling in the desert and they were hungry. Then God sent flakes of bread to rain down each day to sustain the people.[1] Some may read the story of manna from heaven found in the Jewish scriptures and decide the bread landing on people's heads was either an invention of the imagination or a physical phenomenon. Others, including the Hebrew people whom the story is about, believe the bread really came from heaven and that heaven is a real place.

Whether or not we believe in God depends on our view of the pond. We can all look at the bread drifting on the water and eat until we are full and still come to different conclusions as to where it came from. Some see it as evidence of the divine. Others don't. There are many who feel Christianity is superstitious and irrational. In other words, they feel those who cling to science must reject any belief in God The idea goes like this:

> Religious people are dumb.
> Scientific people are smart.

However, I don't think this distinction is correct. It is not that the priest is irrational and the scientist is rational. It is not a conflict between religion and science. The irrational person is the one who claims to know everything (whether religious or scientific). The rational person is the one who is humble and who recognizes there is mystery to the universe.

It is not irrational to believe that God exists or that heaven is real. It is, however, irrational to claim to know everything about this God and the unseen realm he occupies, because no one possesses that much knowledge. Similarly, it is not irrational to have doubts about the existence of God. But it is irrational to claim to know for certain God does not exist and that the minds of men and women will one day answer every question of the universe. Here is another way to phrase this:

> Pride leads to irrational thinking.
> Humility leads to rational thinking.

By this measure, Christians should be extremely rational people, because if there is one trait that dominated Jesus' life, it was humility.

CHAPTER 5

MUD PEOPLE

There are some Christians who are irrational.

Christians believe God created the universe and that God actually interacts with the universe in specific and miraculous ways. Furthermore, Christians believe it is possible to know this God. While I do believe one must apply faith to accept these things, I do not believe it is irrational to believe that God exists, that he can make things, or that he can interact with the things he has made. Neither is it irrational to believe that people can grow in knowledge of this God. But Christianity does become irrational when Christians claim a complete knowledge of the divine and his actions. When a Christian claims to fully grasp how creation unfolded or to fully understand the anatomy of a miracle, this Christian has passed into the realm of irrationality.

Heather and I used to work at a Bible camp in Wisconsin. One morning I was sitting on a wooden bench under the open-air chapel near the edge of camp. I was looking up at a friend of mine who also worked at the camp. The space between us increased as the conversation elapsed. I was agitated with him for suggesting he was open to the possibility of evolution. I rebuked him, stating it was not possible for a Christian to maintain his religion and still entertain the theory of evolution. He tried to explain how his dad was a science teacher and still a Christian. The reason I argued with my friend at the camp was because I was confident in my understanding of the ways in which God enacted creation. I thought to speak of science was to blaspheme God. To acknowledge the things of earth was to cancel out the validity of heaven. I rejected the possibility God could have chosen to act in a way that was beyond my understanding.

In addition to claiming to know how God built the universe, some Christians propose to know exactly how he interacts with it. For example, I have known Christians who suggest that medicine is only for the weak and that the one who swallows a pill renounces his or her faith. In other words, the only answer in the face of sickness is a specific, miraculous healing, because everything else is in opposition to God and should be rejected. I have known people who refused to take medication prescribed by a doctor for fear it would be viewed as an act of faithlessness. When the illness didn't leave, they were told it was because they weren't praying hard enough. I have also heard of people who rejected available cancer treatments and chose instead to fly to a foreign country in search of a faith healer or renowned miracle worker.

I am not criticizing prayer—I fully believe in its power. The danger is when we claim to know not only how God works, but also how he doesn't. I thought knew God wouldn't use some form of evolution to bring about his creation. Others claim to know that God doesn't use doctors or medicine to heal people. But is this rational?

The Bible begins with a story of creation. We are told there was a deep void—an abundance of nothingness. The Spirit of God hovered over black waters. I imagine a mist rising like steam off a muddy river. Then, God spoke a simple phrase: "Let there be light." There was an explosion. A billion particles of light rolled off the tongue of God in a cloud of heat, and the darkness disintegrated. The story continues and creation grows in complexity. It reads like a sheet of music. The pace and pitch of the notes swell to a peak, at which time the breath of God passed into the mouth of the man he shaped out of the mud. And this same breath passed into the mouth of a woman he made from the side of the man. Their lungs were filled with air, and their bodies were filled with the Spirit of God—the same Spirit that hovered over the waters and initiated creation.[1]

Some will read this account and believe that the only possible interpretation is the literal one. On day one light was created, on day two God pulled apart the fabric of creation to create sky and water, and so forth. The story is no deeper than the words used to tell it.

I believe God did create the universe and that the story could have unfolded as a literal interpretation of the Genesis account would suggest. I do not doubt that the audible voice of God actually blasted across the waters, creating a massive wave that vaporized in the heat of the first light. I do not doubt the mud of the earth actually squished through the fingers of God as he built a torso and attached arms and legs to it. And I do not doubt that God could accomplish this in six days.

But neither do I doubt God could have created light and life in some other way and the Genesis account is giving us an illustration of that other way. Some have recognized that the beautiful creation account is actually a poem. It contains a complex structure of repeating words, is built in patterns, and is carried forward by a resounding refrain: "And there was evening, and there was morning—the first day ..."[2]

To suggest that this story is a poem is not to suggest that it is untrue. Writers use poetry all the time to convey true events. One of my favorite songs as a kid was a ballad about the *SS Edmund Fitzgerald* written by Gordon Lightfoot. A simple melody carries through seven or eight verses, and the song basically recounts the events surrounding the demise of an iron ore ship on Lake Superior. The song includes facts. It happened in November. There were twenty-nine men who died. But this factual information was far more compelling because it was tangled up in meter, rhyme, and melody.

So why tell the creation story in the form of poetry? Perhaps it was because poetry has the ability to do more than convey facts. It has the ability to convey truths that are too vast or complex or beautiful for the human mind. The reality is, we could never grasp or understand how light began to burn out of darkness. We could never comprehend how human flesh, which courses with blood, was shaped out of mud the way a sculpture folds out a piece of clay. But a poem can communicate this to us. The beautiful account of Genesis gives a metaphor for some deep reality that we cannot even visualize. Perhaps the process of creation was more complex than we can reach, and so God used a poem to illustrate the true events of this mystery.

The human cell is the most amazing specimen in the material world. In describing what takes place in the cell, American author and professor David Berlinski said it is as if "a cathedral were seen suddenly to rise from the head of a carrot." It is actually impossible to get away from metaphors when talking about the cell, because it is unlike anything else in the physical world.[3] The fact that we are composed of billions of tiny machines with the ability to make more of themselves is beyond comprehension. A human being begins as two single cells join. And from this simple union arises a complexity that results in a newborn child who will emerge to drink air into tiny lungs. The same pattern of increased complexity illustrated in the Genesis story can be seen in nature.

I am not saying I believe God used evolution to bring about creation. What I am trying to say is that I cannot claim to know how God enacted creation. God could have literally voiced all life into existence in less than a week. Or God could have beckoned life into existence through some vast and brilliant blueprint folded into the microscopic boundary of a cell. Or he could have made the world in a million other ways.

If God did make the universe, I also believe he could interact with it in ways that are vast and mysterious.

The Bible is filled with stories of the miraculous. These miracles are unique and varied, and yet there is a common theme in the biblical stories. There is a tangible action on the part of God. This action brings about a result that would not happen under "normal" circumstances. Consider the following set of examples.

- Jesus once spit on the ground to make mud with his saliva. Then he took the mud, spread it on a man's eyes, and told him to go and wash in the Pool of Siloam. The man did as Jesus said and he was given sight.[4]

- In another instance, Jesus healed two blind men by touching their eyes.[5]

- And yet another time Jesus simply spoke and a blind man was able to see.[6]

Though the miracles were varied, they all involved definitive, tangible action on the part of Jesus, who, according to the gospels, was empowered by the Holy Spirit. He spit or he touched or he spoke to bring about the healing.

I believe these stories recorded in the gospels. I also believe miracles of this sort continue to occur in our world—by this I mean miracles that involve a specific divine act that alters creation. As I said, I believe firmly in prayer and in a God who heals people. James tells us to lay hands on one another and pray for the sick. There are countless biblical accounts of the Spirit of God passing through the fingers of common men and women to remove sickness and restore health—just as Jesus did. And there are modern accounts as well. Angus Buchan, a preaching farmer from South Africa, told about a night some woman from a local tribe came to his house screaming. They called him out in a storm, pleading that he come with them to see the woman, who'd been hit by lightning. She was lying in a hut, dead under a blanket. Buchan asked for the woman to be placed in his truck so he could transport her to the hospital. They insisted he pray for her instead. In a simple prayer of faith, the farmer lifted the woman to her feet, and her eyes opened.[7]

I am not suggesting that stories like the biblical accounts or their modern counterparts provide firm evidence for miracles or that someone who is skeptical would be easily convinced by these stories. I am saying there are people who testify to witnessing the miraculous, and I personally believe them. Yet while I believe it is fully possible for God to heal in these ways, I don't believe his healing is limited to these methods. God's actions in the world are much broader.

I saw a story on TV of a father who had been in a car accident and was paralyzed below the neck. One of his deep joys was to play sports with his kids. After the accident, he couldn't pitch a baseball to his son anymore. The producers of the show brought on a team of engineers and designers who built a pitching machine that was controlled by what they called "sip and puff technology." By blowing into a straw, this father was able to operate a pitching machine and play ball with his son again.

Then there is Dr. Ben Carson. The film, *Gifted Hands*, was made about his life. This man is a brilliant brain surgeon. The film drives toward a monumental scene in which Dr. Carson performed surgery on conjoined twins. Their skulls were fused together, and their nerve endings were tied in knots. Carson determined that the only way to perform the surgery would be to stop the twins' hearts. In doing so, he gave himself a fleshy stopwatch by which he was forced to time his surgery. Too much time without a beating heart and the children would die. As classical music pushed the tense air around the room and the hearts of the two children sat frozen, this man separated the mass of tissue that was two human brains. In the end, the doctors pulled the beds apart, and the children rested on their pillows, alive.

These amazing and beautiful acts were conceived by human minds and carried out by human hands. But are they not still miraculous? That God could create an organ inside the human skull which is capable of understanding and performing such healing is amazing. It reminds me of a machine I saw at a health fair. A new hospital opened in our town, and the community was invited to come and see the facility. We actually got to touch a piece of equipment used in advanced surgeries. The operator controls two joysticks that move robotic arms to pick up and manipulate various instruments. I wonder if God can't use our hands to perform healing in the same way.

There are some who will read this and feel a resistance to it. The suggestion that God is mysterious is not always well received. I think this happens for a few reasons. First, Christians desire to know God. This is a good desire and a worthy aim. But sometimes we determine that knowing God means knowing everything about God.

This is not the case. Knowing God doesn't mean we have a complete handle on him. It doesn't mean we can master him or that we can fit all the knowledge of heaven in our heads. If we think we can, we have fallen to pride. Seeking to know God is an act of getting closer to God, not an act of conquering him.

The other reason some Christians resist acknowledging the mystery of God is because it can sound like a cop-out rather than an argument. It sounds like a way to avoid having to prove God. The problem is that attempts to prove or disprove God never end conclusively. There is never a winner in those discussions. Just as there are Christians who are convinced they can prove God exists, there are non-Christians who are equally confident in their ability to prove he doesn't.

CHAPTER 6

INFINITY PLUS ONE

There are many who are certain God does not exist.

Christians are not the only individuals who have been subject to irrational thinking. The antithesis of the irrational Christian is the irrational atheist. The irrational atheist does not necessarily claim to know everything about the universe. But he or she does claim to know God does not exist, confident that the scientific process will one day provide all answers to the mysteries of the universe. He or she is also seeking to remove mystery, but from a different angle. Rather than eliminating mystery by explaining God, the irrational atheist is seeking to eliminate mystery by explaining the universe and therefore removing the need for God.

For much of history, many predominate scientists also believed in God. But a shift in thinking occurred at some point. Religion became synonymous with superstition. It was sometime after this shift that an influential man was born. His life helped perpetuate the movement to remove God. His name was Charles Darwin.

From what I've read of him, I believe Charles Darwin was an intelligent and good-natured man. However, I also believe that he was irrational. He proposed to offer an answer to one of humanity's deepest questions: the question of our origin. He initially provided a picture of how he believed all biological life forms stemmed from an isolated living cell. Then he wrote a second book to illustrate how humanity fit into his picture. The overarching goal was to provide an explanation that did not require any action on the part of God.

In trying to explain how humanity had evolved, Darwin was faced with the problem that human beings are so vastly different from any other living element of the material universe. In an attempt to cross this gap, Darwin tried to elevate animal intelligence while also devaluing human intelligence for certain racial groups. By intelligence I mean the innate ability to learn and process information. It was like he had a rope in each hand. He was trying to pull the two ends together to meet in the middle, stretching both of them to the point of breaking. Listen to what he wrote in the *Descent of Man*.

> At some future period, not very distant as measured by centuries, the civilised races of man will almost certainly exterminate, and replace, the savage races throughout the world ... The break between man and his nearest allies will then be wider, for it will intervene between man in a more civilized state, as we may hope, than the Caucasion, and some ape as low as a baboon, instead of as now between the negro or Australian and the gorilla.[1]

If I hadn't read that myself, I wouldn't believe it. The view being expressed here is that certain races of human beings are closer to animals in their thinking. That passage is usually not included in biology textbooks, but it was the foundation of his argument. When Darwin set out to rank the races, I believe he completely missed humanity. Look at the histories of people on any continent and you will see ingenuity and invention. Both in Darwin's time and in ours, there are groups who live in isolation from the world to some extent. Sometimes this is voluntary. Groups may resist advancement for cultural or moral reasons. Darwin saw a different way of life and assumed those people possessed less intelligence. His thinking reflected the thinking of his time, but it was still flawed.

Imagine for a moment that Darwin had an identical twin—an exact match in looks and brain capacity. And let's imagine this twin was separated at birth from Darwin and was shipped to the Galapagos Islands. The twin was left there as an infant to fend for himself. He grew up with only finches for friends and turtles for parents.

Darwin's twin would never learn to speak or read. He would never follow his grandfather around, soaking in ideas of evolution like his brother. But he was still Charles Darwin's twin—no less intelligent, no less human. Now, if European Darwin showed up in a boat and ran into wild, Galapagos Darwin, he would have classified him as a member of a savage race, a species not much higher than an ape. That seems ironic to me—even irrational. But Darwin had committed to a view of the earth that allowed no room for God.

For his part, Darwin did openly acknowledge there were holes in his theory that would need to be filled in. But he had complete confidence science would provide the answers in the future. He said, "On these grounds I drop my anchor, and believe that the difficulties will slowly disappear."[2] Darwin held the general belief that human intelligence is evolving and will continue to evolve until the human being possesses complete scientific knowledge. In other words, humanity will one day master the universe.

Modern-day skeptic and evolutionist Michael Shermer agrees. He wrote, "Darwin's original claim of evolution by means of natural selection was an extraordinary claim in its time, so he was required to provide extraordinary evidence for it. He did, and evidence has continued accumulating ever since."[3] Shermer is confident that Darwin and those who have adopted his cause have provided solid evidence for their theory. He, like his hero, did admit there are some real questions still to be answered, but he believes science alone will provide the answers.

In his book *Why Darwin Matters*, he identified the following two questions (among others):

- What is the origin of organic molecules?

- How much of modern human behavior can be explained by our evolutionary history?[4]

I find these questions interesting, because these are the same questions Darwin proposed to answer in writing *The Origin of Species* and *The Descent of Man*. In other words, we are wondering how life began and where the human mind and soul came from. It would appear the questions Darwin set out to answer are at least still up for discussion, even for evolutionary scientists. While modern atheists are willing to acknowledge that the questions exist, they are not willing to acknowledge the possibility that God exists as well.

Comedian Ben Stein once interviewed well-known biologist and atheist Richard Dawkins. Stein asked Dawkins about the possibility that life was designed. Dawkins responded by agreeing that microbiologists today are finding what could be called a "signature of some sort of designer." He went on to clarify that he believes this designer would have been created by a process similar to Darwinian evolution. He envisioned a civilization that had evolved to an advanced level and then "seeded" life on this planet.[5] Dawkins remains open to the idea of life having been created. But he seems to have found a creator he is comfortable with—namely, another material being with mega intelligence. The problem is simple. If this being was formed through Darwinian evolution on some distant planet, we may ask, "How did life start on that planet?" Eventually, we are going to run out of planets.

So how did humanity and the universe that holds us come to be? And does science alone have the power to someday answer this question?

Imagine yourself in the Library of Congress. You walk to a back corner of the library and see a little old lady at a small desk. She is punching at a typewriter. After a few minutes of punching, she pulls the page from the machine, sticks it in a folder, and walks over to a tall file cabinet that is tilting to one side. The little old lady drops the folder into the top drawer, picks up a mug that was resting on the file cabinet, and slurps the coffee drip off the side of the mug. Coffee in hand, she walks toward the exit, punches her time card, and disappears.

You walk up to the file cabinet, pulled by curiosity. On the front is an old piece of tape curling at the corners. On the piece of tape you read the word "UNIVERSE." You open the top drawer and pull out the first file. It has today's date. As you begin to read you find that it contains a collection of events. "It rained in Cincinnati." "The president of Iran visited the UN." You quickly realize it is a record of all of the events that occurred today (in very tiny font). Intrigued, you grab the second file and find it has yesterday's date. Flipping backward through these files you realize you are moving backward through history, one day at a time. After reading about Watergate, a very curious thought strikes you. How far back do the files actually go? You decide to start skipping large sections to jump back through time a bit faster. Even with this faster approach you begin to tire. You decide to stop and consider all of this for a moment. How old is the universe?

This is a question scientists have chased forever. Those who study the universe inevitably discuss the idea of entropy. Entropy has to do with order. Things in the universe generally move from a state of order to a state of chaos when left on their own. In other words, things wind down and fall apart and burn out. If you want to change the direction of this and keep something going, you have to apply outside energy to it.

There doesn't seem to be anything in the material universe that can last forever. Energy always has to come from an outside source. This means that each event in the file cabinet must have a previous cause. And as a result, some have come to the conclusion that the files in the drawer go back forever. In other words, the universe never had a beginning—it is infinite.

Infinity is not a number. The simplest way to discuss infinity is by using set theory. A set is a group. So think about strings on a guitar. The set containing all the strings on a guitar would have six members. With sets, you can always count the exact number of members.

When we look at infinity, things change.

An actual infinite set is the set that includes all actual numbers. It has no beginning or end. You can't count the number of members in an infinite set.[6] No matter how far you counted, you would still always have an infinite set of numbers left to count. Imagine a number line stretching in both directions forever. If you started walking along that line, you could never reach the end or even make any progress. If you stopped to rest and looked ahead, you would still have infinity before you.

If this were applied to the history of the universe, we would say that the universe has existed for an infinite number of days or that an infinite series of events has taken place. The assumption of the infinite universe is that it has always existed. There is an infinite past, and the events leading up to today cannot be counted. The question is whether or not this is possible. Another thought experiment may be helpful.

Imagine this time you are camping in Antarctica. While you are trying to build a fire you hear a sifting sound, like something scraping across ice. Looking up, you see a man with a beard down to his ankles coming toward you. It is clear the man has been walking for a while. He stops next to you, and the two of you have the following conversation.

YOU: How long you been walking for?

BEARDED MAN: Forever.

YOU: No, really.

BEARDED MAN: Really, I have been walking forever. I have always been walking. I have taken an infinite number of steps across the unending, frigid wasteland.

YOU: I don't believe you.

BEARDED MAN: I can prove it. I left tracks.

The man points behind him to the footprints in the snow. Intrigued, you start retracing his steps. At any point you can look down and see you've retraced a specific number of steps. But when you look up, you realize you still have an infinite number of steps to go. No matter how far you go, you will always have infinity ahead of you. You might as well be walking on a treadmill because you can't make any ground. Even if you had all the time in the world, even if you could live forever, you could never retrace those steps. And now the problem with his story becomes clear.

For each step he took, there is a footprint. And if there is a footprint, you should be able to count it. If you can count all of the footprints, than there isn't an infinite number of them. And if you can't count them, not even with all the time in the world, then how did he make the footprints in the first place?

That is a good question. And it is a question that has led many to go back to the file cabinet in search of another explanation.

If the files don't go back forever, there must be a first file, and if there was a first file, what would it say? The majority of scientists today would tell us that the first file simply says, "BOOM!" Edwin Hubble discovered something known as redshift as he looked out at the universe. This led him to believe that the universe was expanding.[7] Today this is referred to as the big bang theory. The claim is that all matter and energy in the universe were once condensed into something less than a single point (referred to as a singularity). Edgar Andrews clarifies that this should be thought of not as an explosion, but more like an expansion. He used the analogy of blowing up a balloon.[8] It made me think of the time my college roommate and I put one of those marshmallow rabbits you see at Easter in the microwave. As it expanded, each little grain of yellow sugar moved farther away from all the other little grains of sugar. Of course, in our experiment, the bunny burst into flames. Thankfully, this hasn't happened to the universe yet.

There are many who support the big bang theory, and many who feel it provides a beginning for our universe. As with anything in science, some are doubtful. Professor David Berlinski wrote an article about the big bang in which he references a mathematician named

I. E. Segal. Segal has sharply criticized Hubble's idea of redshift, which is the basis for the theory.[9]

Currently, the most widely accepted theory is the big bang. But if it is true, we have another problem. The claim is that the universe was once a single point. So instead of being infinitely large, it was infinitely small. But how does that work? We are right back at the problems with infinity as a math problem versus infinity in the real world.

I should mention another popular theory, known as the oscillating big bang. This theory suggests that the universe is in a constant pattern of contracting and expanding. So there have been many bangs.[10] This theory doesn't seem to help us with the infinity problem. Instead of going infinitely large or infinitely small, it does both—over and over again.

Regardless of whether the universe is frozen, expanding, or doing cartwheels, we are still looking for an answer as to how it began. It feels like infinity is inevitable, but it also seems it is impossible. There is one option remaining, however. It is possible infinity is a real phenomenon but that it does not describe our universe. Instead, our universe is a finite reality within a larger infinite reality. There is something else that exists independently of this universe that caused us to be here. In other words, the first file says, "See other file cabinet."

There are now scientists starting to think outside this universe. They use terms like "multiverse" and "bubble universe." The thought is that a universe such as ours could be an offshoot of some other universe. It either is sprouting off the side of another universe or emerged from a black hole within that universe. Some suggest that a highly intelligent species from one of these alternate universes could have engineered ours. Others believe there are an infinite number of universes and that the process of a new universe forming is a spontaneous result of evolution on a massive scale. In any case, the proponents of the multiverse theory will suggest that these other universes are similar to ours in that they are material (i.e., composed of some form of matter and energy).

The goal here, I think, is to show that there could be something beyond our universe that accounts for our being here while keeping things within the reach of science. Though the multiverse theory has become popular, it has its opponents within the academic realm. David Berlinski, a man who seems to keep a healthy skepticism for just about all scientific theories, comments, "There is, needless to say, no evidence whatsoever in favor of this preposterous theory."[11] His point is simple. If alternate material universes exist, they would be beyond the reach of science simply because they reside beyond our reality. This theory sounds scientific, but science is limited to things that can be observed and cataloged and measured—things we can touch.

If the universe is infinitely large, there are times and spaces we will never reach and cannot analyze. If the universe is infinitely small and came from nothing, we could never fully explain the origin, because nothing is nothing—what would we have to observe? And if there was a cause to our universe, it must be placed outside our universe and therefore beyond our reach. English writer G. K. Chesterton said, "The poet only asks to get his head into the heavens. It is the logician who seeks to get the heavens into his head. And it is his head that splits."[12]

See the irrational atheist makes the same mistake as the irrational Christian. Each claims to have access to this vast bank of knowledge that is actually too great for any person to hold in his or her head. It is irrational for both the Christian and the atheist to claim so much knowledge. Such claims are prideful. It could be said that pride leads to irrational thinking. It leads to a distorted view of oneself and of reality. And if pride leads to irrationality, perhaps humility can do the opposite.

CHAPTER 7

SMALL NEXT TO GOD

Christianity is a rational religion.

This sounds odd because of our understanding of the word rational. We associate rational thinking with science. By this measure any belief in God seems irrational. But we have already seen that the atheist scientist is also capable of being irrational. The rational person is not the one who claims to know much, but one who can admit to knowing little, the one who is okay with being small like a child, and the one who is humble. To see this, we must first understand humility. Then we can see how humility leads to wisdom. And if we want to understand humility, we must look at Jesus.

One may question the suggestion that Jesus was humble when considering that he claimed to be God. In the gospel of John, Jesus was speaking to a group of Jewish leaders. He told them, "You are from below; I am from above. You are of this world; I am not of this world."[1] Here and in other places, Jesus told people that he had a divine origin. Many would hear this and think it an arrogant and irrational claim. We have seen other leaders turn themselves into deities in their own imaginations. Some built giant tombs guarded by thousands of stone soldiers. Others hired writers to draft their biographies, trying to ensure they would remain immortal in the hearts of their subjects. There have been many kings who seemed to believe themselves to be gods. For a person to claim he or she is God is arrogant—unless it is true. If it is true then it would not be arrogant at all. And in looking at his life through the stories told about him, humility emerges as one of Jesus' most obvious traits. This is clear from the time he was born—because of the way he came.

Many are familiar with the story of Jesus' birth. We see the nativity as a cute scene we set up once a year. But the true story of his coming involves far more struggle and discomfort than we often acknowledge.

When our first son was born, the nativity story gained ground in my heart. The night we brought Samuel home, we could hear the neighbor through the walls of our townhouse. His boy was screaming as he yelled at his wife. There was the sound of things breaking—a picture frame, maybe. I almost called the police. Then I looked at my wife and son, and the whole thing seemed fragile. I hoped to God I could protect them.

Heather's body had been through trauma due to the rapid delivery. Within those first days, she became severely dehydrated and had to go to the emergency room. Two couples we knew came to watch Samuel while I took Heather to the hospital in the middle of the night. He was a few days old, and we couldn't expose him to the emergency room. If not for those beautiful people, I'm not sure what would have happened.

We sat for four hours on the stiff seats of the ER admittance room. The details are a fog. All those hospital rooms started to look the same. I do remember a man who was rushed in. He was bleeding from somewhere. I wondered if he'd been in a knife fight, or maybe he drank too much and tripped over a lamp.

Heather leaned on me, trying to find rest. You wouldn't know it was the middle of the night outside. The cold light falling from the ceiling was unforgiving, as though we were specimens in a lab. Everything felt sterile and yet filthy, as though an invisible epidemic was crawling through the room. It tore at me that my wife was sitting there. It was not a place for a new mom in need of peace and rest.

The tension began to slowly unravel, but it took time. Following the night in the ER, my mom flew in from Minneapolis to help. She arrived as I was leaving the hospital to go pick up Samuel from the saints who were caring for him. When we got to their house, there was peace resting on everything. Samuel was warm and sleeping on several blankets. In a moment of creativity born out of necessity, they'd made his bed in a laundry basket. When I look back on all this, that laundry basket reminds me of a manger.

When we think of a manger we may see a crisp wooden box cut from cedar, smelling like saw dust and cinnamon and lined with goose down. Think instead of a stone trough. Also think about being surrounded

SMALL NEXT TO GOD

by animals. Have you watched cows feed? They chew up corn or straw mixed with dirt. Strings of saliva hang from their nostrils as they grind the feed into sludge. Flies bounce back and forth from the faces of the animals to the feed box. The insects land on an ear or an eyelid, and the cows just keep grinding and drooling as they eat their muddy meals.

What about the stable? We see a quaint, red barn sitting on a hillside. The animals were probably kept in a cave rather than a man-made structure, and if you have been around a barn or some sort of shelter for animals, you are familiar with the dominant smell. We took our kids to the county fair and walked in and out of the animal buildings. The moment we exited one building, the breeze would carry fresh air to our lungs, a small act of redemption before we entered the next pole barn. Animal waste and wet straw covered the floor. The giant utility fans blowing everywhere could not cut the heavy air. Instead, they just caused the smell to swirl and bounce off the walls.

And Bethlehem—a quiet little town with adobe buildings and stars pinned to the sky? No. Shortly after Jesus was born, Bethlehem became the target of a bloody infanticide. The king of that region sent his militia to slaughter every baby boy under two years of age. The Jewish people were occupied by the Roman hand, and the Jewish kings were the corrupt fingers of that hand.

If there is one word to describe the way in which the gospel writers speak of Jesus' arrival, it is humble. The writer of Philippians tells us Jesus did not consider equality with God something to be grasped. Instead, he gave it up.[2] I have no clue how this could happen—God becoming human. It seems this would involve a stripping down, a shedding, a reduction—infinity now bound by time and a body. Once God arrived in human form, he behaved in a way that was different from what many would have expected.

Jesus waited almost three decades to reveal he was from God—which also speaks to his humility. That is a big thing to keep quiet for thirty years. Once it was time to share his identity, he began to preach and heal people, wielding incredible miracles. It was not just the blind receiving their site or skin disease falling off of bodies. We are told thousands of hungry people were fed from a few loaves of bread. Demons were hurled out of people. Jesus' friends watched as he walked across the surface of the water toward their boat. Dead people came back to life, sat up, and began to walk around.

Despite this display of amazing power, the most common instruction Jesus gave to those who witnessed it was to remain quiet about what they had seen. After Jesus healed a blind man, he told him to go straight home rather than enter the village, where people would recognize the evidence of a miracle.[3] And though he spent time with the masses while carrying out this ministry, he often moved to quiet places of solitude. There was even an instance when Jesus evaded a crowd of people who came to make him king by force after witnessing his abilities.[4] Jesus could have capitalized on his power. He could have secured his fame. Instead he seemed to make himself small and obscure. And we can see the same pattern in his teaching.

The biographers of Jesus tell us over and again that he amazed people with his wisdom. As a young boy he sat among a company of wise men in the temple and perplexed them with his understanding.[5] The people in his hometown were astounded by the wisdom of his teaching.[6] He even silenced his challengers during debates—to the point where they didn't dare ask him anymore questions.[7] He seemed to possess a wisdom that came from somewhere else. The other teachers appealed to an outside authority. But Jesus taught under his own authority.

If Jesus is God, then he possesses greater knowledge than any man. His knowing ignores the rules of time. The past that has faded to nothing is visible to him. He has access to eternity. He is a fellow citizen of angels and engages in hand-to-hand combat with demons. He even sits upon the seat of heaven. The Bible also teaches that Jesus was present when the universe was built.[8] He assisted in the assembly of creation. And he understands the natural laws of science because he helped write them. In the Old Testament book of Job, God asks Job if he was present when the footings of the world were poured and when the edges of the universe were measured off.[9] Jesus, according to the Bible, was there. All of this knowledge is contained within his mind.

But despite possessing this knowledge, Jesus seemed to surrender or forfeit something at the point of incarnation. He often deferred to God when asked questions. He said, "I do nothing on my own but speak just what the Father has taught me."[10] When asked about when the earth would burn to the ground and heaven would come crashing down, Jesus said only the Father knew the time and the day.[11] And Jesus repeatedly made it clear that the things he taught were told to him by his Father. Though he was one with God, he seemed to willingly take a place of submission and humility.

You may be wondering what a lengthy theological discussion about Jesus' humility actually proves. All I am trying to illustrate is that the first followers of Jesus had a certain perception of him. This perception emerged from their encounters with Jesus. And based on what they wrote, it is clear they perceived him to be a man of great humility. While other kings desired more knowledge and power and understanding, Jesus possessed all of it and chose to release his grip. He laid it down. And by this example he directed his followers to do the same. For many of us this seems counterproductive. How can I become wiser by admitting that I am a fool? How can humility grant me a greater understanding of reality? How does being humble make me more rational? It is simple: if we acknowledge we don't know everything, we have room to receive more knowledge.

The one who is humble is the one who is willing to listen. He recognizes that there is some vacancy in his mind and therefore room to learn more. She doesn't deny the existence of something she doesn't understand. He doesn't belittle the things he can't comprehend. And she doesn't seek to possess things too great for her. The humble person is okay with appearing small next to God.

This doesn't mean we don't pursue knowledge. This is not an exercise in passivity. We should not just lie back like an open lid on a garbage can and wait for knowledge to descend. We should be eager to grow in wisdom. For Jesus also said he would be found by those who seek him.[12] We just need to recognize our limits in the process.

We can draw precise topographical maps and measure mountains. But this does not explain why some of us possess an inner fire that compels us to cling to the face of a rock with only a rope around our waists. We can comprehend the development of a human embryo and perform emergency surgeries that save two lives at once. But this does not explain why a mother will forget the pain of childbirth as soon as her baby is resting in the crease of her elbow. We can design aircrafts that cut through the atmosphere like flying kitchen knives. But this does not explain why some of us long to fly and others maintain a fear of heights.

In other words, it is possible to be both a scientist and a priest. It is possible to value knowledge and embrace the mystery of God. Chesterton said, "Mysticism keeps men sane. As long as you have mystery you have health, when you destroy mystery you create morbidity … It is exactly this balance of apparent contradictions that has been the whole buoyancy of the healthy man."[13] We could exchange the word healthy for the word rational.

There is another implication to choosing humility. It seems God chooses to reveal himself to the humble.

We are told that God stands in opposition to the proud and offers the relief of grace to the humble.[14] The prophet Isaiah issued a warning to those who are wise in their own eyes.[15] And Jesus said God has chosen to hide things from the self-proclaimed wise ones and reveal them to little children.[16]

What specifically does God reveal to those who approach him like little children? God reveals himself. He did this in the person of Jesus.

The Bible says the word (meaning Jesus) became flesh and that he was the image of the invisible God.[17] He laughed and cried and ate food. He came to be with us and to reveal himself to those who would be willing to have enough humility to see him. This is the claim of Christianity.

But this does raise an important question. No person living today was allowed to witness the events recorded in the Gospels. And beyond that, there are many who have never even heard of the Gospels or of this man Jesus. So what of them? Has God used any other means to reveal himself? Is there any other evidence that could bring us to know this God? As we consider the experiences of our own lives and the collective experiences of humanity, can we find evidence of the divine? I believe we can.

CHAPTER 8

DON'T EAT SAND

The world is filled with the evidence of God.

There is no definitive proof that God exists—not in the scientific sense of the word. If God exists, he cannot be weighed or measured or charted. But when we release our insistence on acquiring proof and just consider the reality of our experiences, I believe traces of the divine can be seen everywhere.

I was reading the back cover of a book written by a man who claimed he could provide absolute proof of God's existence. I am not sure how he pulled that one off. I didn't read it because I don't believe God can fit in a book. One of the most common tactics used to measure or "prove" God's existence relates to probability. People will perform calculations that illustrate how vastly unlikely it would have been for life to spontaneously generate from the mud. They then slide to the natural conclusion that these calculations also prove God.

I remember learning about probability in math class. The first example that always comes to mind relates to socks. If I have one blue sock and two red socks in my drawer, what is the probability I will pull out a blue sock without looking in the drawer? And the answer comes quickly. I have a one-in-three chance, or about a thirty-three percent probability, of grabbing the blue sock. This is because there are three socks in the drawer, and one of them is blue. Easy enough. That is probability.

Chevy Chase made a movie years back called *Christmas Vacation*. When his great-aunt arrived at the house for Christmas dinner, she was carrying presents. They were actually just things from around her house that she wrapped up to give away. One of the boxes was shaking and meowing. It turned out to be her cat. So if you were to come up to a box that was moving and making catlike noises, you may say to the person next to you, "What are the chances there is a cat in that box?"

But you would find the person couldn't give an easy answer like "I think there is a fifty percent chance." The reason an easy answer wouldn't come is because it is not a probability question. There is either a cat in the box or there isn't a cat in the box. Probability doesn't factor in.

There are certain questions where probability doesn't help—we'll call them cat-in-the-box questions. And the question of God's existence is a cat-in-the-box question. We cannot assign numbers and statistics to the question of God's existence. But we can sit still and look at the box. And our experience of that box may reveal to us whether it is reasonable to conclude that there is a cat inside. Based on my experiences, I believe there is a cat in the box. But what does it mean to experience God?

Have you ever lost something in the ocean? The search is menacing. You may know the feeling of raking the sand with your toes for something that feels like a wedding ring or a pocket knife. If you reach down to grab what you think is the lost item, a large wave will invariably rise to smack you in the head and fill your ear canal with saltwater. Searching for God is just the opposite of this. Instead of God being the ring or the knife, he is the ocean or the sand. God can be difficult to grab hold of, not because he is hidden or lost, but because he is so big. Many religions hold this idea of the otherness of God. The Jewish scriptures (also found in the Old Testament of the Christian Bible) say God's thoughts outnumber the grains of sand on the earth. So knowing everything about God would be like counting sand.

We have a sandbox in the yard we built for the boys with the help of their grandparents. We got the sand from a landscaping place, and I hauled it home in a rented pickup truck. It took a long time to shovel that sand into the wooden frame. Some of it didn't make it to the box. It landed in the grass or remained in the grated truck bed or flew out the back of the truck as I was driving through town to return the rental on time. I couldn't ever count each grain of sand in that box. I can't even count the number of grains that end up in the kids' hair after they are done playing.

It is impossible to count sand. But it is possible to know about sand by experiencing it. My experience with sand is very tangible to me.

I can retrieve memories of sitting on the edge of the box with my kids and making waffles or tunnels or mountains—and telling Noah to stop eating the sand. I can feel sand under my bare feet like the night my wife and I were walking on a beach in Virginia. We saw a whale clouding the air with a mist as it paced back and forth like a lap swimmer. I can hear the sound of breath traveling down a pipe, blowing a mass of melted sand into the shape of a glass. And I can study the way that glass bends light and pulls my eyes close together in a distorted reflection. Experiencing sand is better than counting it.

I am suggesting that while we cannot count the thoughts of God or fit heaven into our heads, we can experience the reality of God and feel the breath of heaven.

Speaking about experiencing God can sound very mystical. And it should. If it is possible for a human being to literally encounter the divine, it would be mystical. But our reservation is deeper than that. Talking about using our experiences as evidence of God's existence can sound overly simplistic, unscholarly, and even irrational.

And I understand the risk. If we define reality only by our experiences, we will have a false sense of reality. It may be possible for me to conclude that racism is not real because I have not felt the scourge of a racist insult. But this does not mean racism is not real; it means my experiences are limited. In addition to denying certain realities based on my experiences, I can also invent realities. I may actually experience something but then surrender the experience to the creative energy of my imagination and draw conclusions that weren't there.

Having acknowledged the risks, I still believe our experiences are real and are therefore a valid means by which to measure truth. A. W. Tozer said this of the man who accepts the reality of his experience:

> By the deep wisdom of life he is wiser than a thousand men who doubt. He stands upon the earth and feels the wind and rain in his face and he knows that they are real. He sees the sun by day and the stars by night. He sees the hot lightning play out of the dark thundercloud. He hears the sounds of nature and the cries of human joy and pain. These he knows are real.[1]

The visible can teach us about the invisible. Our experience of this world has something to tell us about a deeper reality. And the more experiences we gain, the sharper the image will become. If we test our experiences against the experiences of others, we can begin to establish a sense of collective experience. This keeps our realities in check by trying to understand and relate to the experiences of others. All of this can help us to see the world for what it really is. If I stop and watch the experiences of my life play out like scenes in a film, I am amazed by what I see.

One of my favorite places in the world is a small hill on the western edge of Wisconsin. It sits miles from any road on the property of Ox Lake Bible Camp. It was a place where we told stories and sang songs as smoke from a fire drifted into the black. One night, we slept on top of that hill and stared at heaven. There is enough space out there that even the distant universal lights can be seen. Stars fell and ran across the sky. The constellations traveled from one edge of the horizon to the other as our tiny hill twirled through space. And though I believe their worship was misplaced, I could understand why many throughout history have believed those stars to be gods.

We recently drove west and pushed our van up a mountain past the timberline. Up there, the air feels wide and clouds implode on themselves.

Trees hold on to the edge of the cliff, and rocks rest scattered and buried in moss. It felt like we were driving up a ramp into heaven. At the top, we sipped at the air and sipped from our water bottles. We were able to see chains of mountains moving north and south, like a giant mole had tunneled across the country. I rested on a bare rock with the sun pressing against my face and closed my eyes. I could feel a continent under my back and a sky over my head and felt a deep peace, realizing I was pressed between the two. It felt good to be that small and to be held by such beauty.

One summer I traveled with a friend and his parents to Canada to go fishing. He and I rode on the bucket seats of his dad's truck. All I remember from the drive is stopping for bad eggs around dawn and then having my knees in my chest for a very long time. The place we stayed was on a peninsula, and there were these tiny lakes everywhere. From a plane, the area would have looked like a street filled with potholes after a rain. One morning we hiked to one of these lakes to fish. We pushed off into the empty water to look for trout. They mostly ignored us. So after floating on the still water for a while we decided to move on to a different lake.

As we got close to the shore I looked up. There, standing ankle-deep at the edge of the lake, was a moose. It was too shallow to drop the motor, so we grabbed the oars to push back out. I had a vision of the moose rushing the boat, flipping it over, and pounding us into a damp grave. We managed to free ourselves and ended up back in the middle of the lake, where we stayed for at least half an hour. The moose stood there the entire time just chewing on grass. From a safe distance I realized she was powerful and beautiful. This majestic animal that could easily kill me stood calm with reeds hanging out the corner of her mouth. Then she quietly left.

The vast beauty I find throughout the world is the clearest when I consider the most amazing element of all creation—human beings. And my deepest experiences of this beauty come from those closest to me.

I have a picture of Heather from when she was very young. She was sitting in a chair next to a screen door. Her lips were drawn tight in a line, and she was holding a pellet gun next to her cheek, with the barrel in the air—the way you would hold a gun if you were hiding behind a tree, waiting for something terrible, like a Velociraptor, to sneak up on you. She was hunting chipmunks. She has gone bungee jumping and skydiving, and she even swam with sharks once. I will come home and find massive pieces of furniture (like a couch or a piano) moved to different rooms of the house. Her hair color changes depending on the time of year, and when it is humid, the hair that frames her face curls like delicate ribbons. She makes bread from scratch and she smells good all the time. She says really cute things, like "I like mallards because they have orange feet." She is not without flaw. But this adds to her beauty. She asks for forgiveness in such a gentle way. And she also gives it freely—which is good, because my flaws are many.

Then there is Samuel pounding on a guitar and singing with all of the breath in his lungs. He weaves intricate stories, pulling details from somewhere that should be out of reach to a five-year-old. He can passionately resist my efforts to steer his course and then throw his arms around my neck to signify an apology. He aspires to be a park ranger and plans to save his money to buy a slingshot or a chainsaw.

Noah entered the story after Samuel. He will run to us through the shadows saying, "It's pretty scary." Then he will lift up his hands, each clutching a matchbox car, and ask to be held. He prefers to avoid any food that is green, and his deep laugh is bigger than his small lungs can contain. He apparently has bones of steel and knees of leather, because he seems to bounce off the ground any time he falls.

Eliana is still very new. A single pigtail stands on the top of her head, pointing to heaven. She will often wave her arms fast enough to gain lift, like she is preparing to fly off the highchair. Even though her arms can't reach around our shoulders, she hugs us hard enough to press the air out of our chests. When we set her in the grass, she lifts both arms and one leg in the air in an attempt to maintain as little contact as possible with the ground. The scratching sensation is still strange on her small toes.

Of course, none of this happens in isolation. The beautiful scenes are tangled together—like the day we were picking strawberries.

I looked to see Heather holding herself up with one hand and pulling at berries with the other. Her hair had blown across her face, thinly covering her eyes, and sunlight ran from her shoulders down to her wrists. Sam was jumping over rows of plants while Noah ate strawberries and rubbed the red juice across his face. Ellie lay next to the field, sleeping in the breeze.

It may sound as though I am taking the ordinary and turning it into the miraculous. And it may seem like a stretch to suggest these experiences point to God. Many atheists have refuted the Christian's attempt to use beauty as evidence for God. But I have witnessed something very interesting. There are some who do not believe in God but still consider these things I have described to be amazing and even miraculous.

J. Craig Ventor is a scientist who was involved in the human genome project. These are the people who helped map the genetic information in the human cell. He is rather smart. I watched him interviewed on *60 Minutes*. Currently, he and his team of highly funded scientists are working to alter genetic information within bacteria to create new species of organisms. At the end of the interview, he was asked if he believed in God. Ventor responded,

> No, I believe the universe is far more wonderful, than just assuming it was made by some higher power. I think the fact that these cells are software driven machines and that software is DNA and that's truly the secret of life is writing software, it's pretty miraculous.[2]

Ventor believes this world is miraculous. He believes life is miraculous. And when I saw the gleam in his eyes as he spoke, I realized he believes these things for the same reasons I have described above. He believes it because the world contains an intricate and amazing beauty. But he doesn't believe in God. The question is, Why? Why have he and others come to such a different conclusion? It is not because he doesn't find creation to be miraculous. It is not irrational to look at the beauty I have described and see evidence of God in it. I don't think that most of us would take account of the beautiful things in our lives and use those as reasons to dethrone God. These are not the experiences that cause us to question God's existence. So what is it?

It is when the mountains flatten into a vast desert or the rains level the trees in a flood that we question. It is when the child revolts or the lover cheats that we doubt. The rejection of God emerges when depression is the heaviest thing around us and it chokes our laughter, or when grass no longer grows because a field has become a mass grave. These experiences are just as real as the others I described. These are the experiences that bring us to raise angry fists toward God.

It is not so much that God can't exist in light of our pain. If God doesn't exist, at least our pain makes sense. What really haunts us when we look at the death around us is a simple question: If God does exist, what kind of God is he?

PART III: IRRELEVANT

Either God wants to abolish evil, and cannot; or he can, but does not want to.

—Epicurus

PART III: IRRELEVANT

My dad used to drive us to school in our minivan. We were driving at least sixty miles per hour one morning on the highway that led to the high school. I was looking out the passenger window of the front seat. Suddenly, I was assaulted by the loudest noise I've ever heard. The world outside the car went fuzzy, and I saw flashes of light and spinning metal, and the sound kept going. Then, suddenly, it was silent; either I'd gone deaf or the world was mute. And I realized I was hanging upside down. I began to smell gasoline and melting rubber. I don't remember actually releasing the seat belt or climbing out of the window that had been shattered. I am not sure how I didn't cut myself on the saw-like shards of glass that outlined the window frame. Nor am I aware of how everyone else got out of the car.

I just remember standing in the ditch next to the van, which looked like a June bug flipped on its back, the tires dangling in the air like legs. Then a kid came running toward our car, holding his head and saying, "Oh my God!" He just kept repeating it. The frantic kid had T-boned us. He pulled onto the highway as we were coming full speed and broadsided the van on the driver side, causing it to roll and eventually rest in the ditch.

I also know of two children who were in a car accident. They were much younger when they were struck—one not old enough to remember. The car they were strapped into was hit by a truck, much like ours was. They lived. Their mother didn't. The two accidents were deeply similar. Why did one bring death and the other didn't? Why did my dad live, and why did their mom die?

Death surrounds us and it influences our conclusions about God. Many see this death and determine that God does not exist at all. This conclusion does help explain the reality of death. If there is no God, it would make sense that nothing makes sense. People die and pain is real, but it has no meaning. Others would insist that God does exist, despite the death we see. If we acknowledge the existence of God, we are faced immediately with a problem. If God exists and death is real, we have to find a way to reconcile this. We have to ask what this God is like.

Some say that God is like a dictator. He is amped up with power and wills every collision and explosion. He is capable of doing away with suffering; he just chooses not to. This God can do without humanity. Our living or dying is as arbitrary as the earthworm dried on the sidewalk after a rain.

Others imagine a God who is more like Nelson Mandela during the years he spent in prison. Mandela was a good leader, and he would later emerge as a great leader. Even from prison he had a powerful influence and inspired so many. But his power to tangibly act was limited—it had been stripped. This type of God is loving and benevolent. He would like to help but he is bound and unable to do so.

If God is powerful, he can't be good, or he would end suffering. If God is good, he can't be powerful, or he would end suffering.

Yet Christians claim their God is good and powerful. They claim God has destroyed death. This would be good news, except to many, this God seems like a phantom or a fable—because they hear Christians talk about eternal life but don't see the results. Death still abounds and the church seems irrelevant. As a result many have come to conclude we must save ourselves.

I don't believe the Christian gospel is a fake. Jesus has destroyed death and restored life to people. Many of us just haven't seen it, and therefore we've missed the life he is offering. Thankfully, it is not too late to find it.

CHAPTER 9

GO BACK TO YOUR OWN NEIGHBORHOOD

Christianity often seems irrelevant.

The core message of Christianity is that Jesus has saved us from death. Many are skeptical of this message because they don't see evidence of this salvation. Often Christians will speak of this promise and move to persuade others to accept it but then have nothing else to offer. This leads many to conclude that the God of Christianity is not relevant.

As a teenager I attended a small Bible study that met in a science classroom once a week. We would gather before school started on Wednesdays. One morning, several members of the group suggested that we reach out to the other students in our school with the message of Jesus. From there, a simple plan was made. We would buy boxes of candy bars in bulk and tape Christian tracts to the packaging. Then we would pass out the gospel candy to students walking into the building in the morning.

I never spoke during the meetings. I just perspired a lot over in a corner. The night before the event I didn't really sleep because of a stomachache. I woke up, got dressed, and drove to school in the dark. There was a box sitting at my station between the first line of glass doors and the second, which opened into the building. The air in my small glass cage fluctuated from cold to hot as the outside doors opened and closed. I stood with my box at my feet and mostly looked down. As I passed out the candy I kept my voice below the hum of the register that breathed against my back.

The time passed quickly. It ended up being somewhat painless. As I think back on it, the other students who had planned this event had good intentions. They were brave and kind people—risking their reputations to do something they believed in. And I believe they really wanted their peers to find life. I don't have a way to confirm whether our form of outreach changed anyone's life. But I do know I didn't actually meet anyone that day. I didn't learn anyone's story. I don't think my actions that day were very relevant to the lives of most of the people who ate my chocolate. I also know this form of evangelism is rather common.

We were driving into Nashville on a Saturday morning. The sun burned against the buildings, pouring light off a thousand windows. Heather steered to the curb, and I got out to see if the visitor center was open, as this was our first time through the city. It was locked, so I walked back to the van, taking pictures of guitars outlined in neon lights and a statue of Elvis.

After I shut the door I looked up and saw a woman walking toward our vehicle. She was making a motion for me to roll down the window. Before Heather had a chance to comment or I had time to think, I hit the button and her words rushed in with the wind.

The woman informed us she was an anointed street preacher and wanted to tell me that the pictures I was taking were worthless. She went on to say that I should take a picture of Nashville with my family in the frame. That picture would be valuable because Jesus had died to give us worth. She ended the conversation by saying her church in St. Louis was the only real church around. After that, she was gone.

This wasn't the first encounter I've had with an evangelist. One time, a man came to my front door to make sure I knew Jesus. He also said I should come to his church (which was not in St. Louis). And back when I was in high school, I knew a kid who stood up on a chair in the cafeteria, cupped his hands around his mouth, and invited everyone to a Christian event he was organizing. When my wife was in college, she saw a man standing in the river holding a staff. He was warning the passing students of their impending damnation.

I have also had experiences where the evangelist took a subtler approach. Once during a parade I was sitting on a curb waiting for a tootsie roll. A man walked by and, without looking at me, placed a small booklet in my hand. The cover had a picture of a cross superimposed on top of the globe. On a different occasion, I was invited to an Easter service at someone's church without ever meeting the person.

He or she left a flyer under the windshield wiper blade as my car sat empty in a parking lot. And surprisingly, one of the most common places I have seen evangelism at work is on the walls of a bathroom stall. Usually it is in response to the other messages carved in the paint.

In all of these experiences, there has been a common theme. Every encounter was rather brief and somewhat impersonal. Nobody talked to me long enough to find out that I was already a Christian. Nobody talked to me long enough to learn my name. In fact, in some cases, nobody talked to me at all. So why does Christian evangelism often look like this?

It is because many have come to believe the goal of Christianity is to escape the flood. And people who are interested staying dry tend to fill sandbags.

There is a view that a flood is covering the world. Buildings are falling over, cars are floating down the street, and people are thrashing and flailing to try to keep their lungs from filling up with water. The world is drowning because of sin and evil, and the church is like a city up on a hill that rises above the flood plain. So the whole goal of the modern church is to help as many people as possible to escape from the flood and get to higher ground before the rescue helicopters come in to take people out of here—in other words, before Jesus comes back. The way to escape from this flood is to believe in Jesus. To use the universal terminology, people need to "accept Jesus as their personal Lord and Savior" (a phrase that does not appear in the Bible as far as I know). As long as they make this determination, they are in the clear.

Within this picture of Christianity, evangelism is fairly simple. You basically need to present a condensed version of the good news and then solicit a response. There isn't really an emphasis placed on getting to know people or investing in their lives, because all you need to do is convince them to make a one-time decision. It's like gathering names for a petition—getting people to say yes to Jesus and ushering their souls into heaven.

I understand what motivates this. It is not that this idea is completely off. But it is vastly incomplete. I believe this world is dying and that Jesus' mission was and is to ransom and redeem people. But redeem them for what purpose? Because of the way Christianity is often presented, many join the church and then don't know what to do. Nothing else really changes—for them or for anyone else around them. The church sometimes seems to lack a sense of purpose, and therefore it lacks the urgency to act. Now that we are up on the hill there is nothing to do but wait. And since we are waiting, we might as well get comfortable.

If you want to sell a Christian book these days, one of the best ways seems to be to tell people that Jesus will make them rich and healthy. Become a Christian and avoid all suffering. Become a Christian and life will be comfortable. Oftentimes the people saying these things are also rich and healthy. So they are living proof it works. I am not seeking to be cynical. This is a simple observation. When a writer or pastor tells people that Christianity is mainly about comfort, they sign up for it. There are two problems with this. First, it isn't true. Let me clarify. I believe the message of Jesus has the power to bring comfort that can shelter us. But it is a comfort that comes in the midst of suffering, not a comfort that removes us from the suffering. Jesus' first followers did not become rich or escape suffering by choosing to follow him—quite the opposite, actually. Additionally, the gospel of comfort is a problem because it doesn't actually lead to life any way. It is an empty promise that leaves people disillusioned and bored.

Comfortable is very appealing at first. It is easier than uncomfortable. My grandma lived in a nursing home in her last few years. My mom made sure she was in a good place and was unyieldingly faithful in spending time with her there. Sometimes I would go with. But in my heart there was always an underlying resistance to going. It was not because I didn't want to see my grandma or because I didn't think it was important. It was because I was uncomfortable around all of that suffering. The people in my grandma's wing of the home were losing their memories—just like her. Some would just stare and others would cry out. One lady constantly muttered cuss words. It was easier to go on with life outside of that place and to try not to think about it.

Much of my Christian life has been spent avoiding discomfort and risk. I have dabbled in discomfort—just enough to feel like I was interacting in the world. I have risked just enough to feel that I needed God for a moment. But often I have avoided the uncomfortable and the daring and chosen instead to sit in clean and comfortable places. This is how many of us live out Christianity. There is an initial decision made to follow Jesus or to accept his salvation, but then there is really nothing that follows.

Though we feel we are securing our lives, we are actually forfeiting something vital: our purpose. And if we don't have a purpose, we can't be relevant. This is how Christianity has become irrelevant. When we decide to sit down and huddle comfortably together, we become insulated from the death around us. This causes us to lose touch. It causes us to become strangers to our neighbors. In this place it becomes impossible to have an impact.

When I was in high school, I went on a bus trip to Washington, DC, with my church. We stopped in Harrisburg, Pennsylvania, to do a few days of mission work. We slept on the floor of a church basement and basically spent our time on various cleanup projects for a local ministry. I remember smashing concrete with a sledgehammer to clean up an empty lot and pulling weeds from the cracks in the cement. One day, our group decided to go on a prayer walk through the neighborhood near the church where we were staying. A prayer walk is where you walk around and pray for people or places as you pass by. They are silent prayers. If someone were to take a solitary prayer walk, nobody would even notice them.

There were twenty or thirty of us. We were kind of mashed together in a mob, moving like a long, slinky dragon in a parade—except our identities were not concealed by colorful folds of silk. As we walked past the rows of houses, people on front porches and curbs stared at us with curiosity or disdain (or both). A teenage kid jumped from his front steps and hit his chest as if to issue a challenge. He blocked the sidewalk, his friends looking on, until he saw those at the front of the group were going to keep walking. He then stepped aside onto the stairs, just enough to allow the mob to squeeze by, staring down his chest at each head that passed.

We turned a corner, and a man drifting through the intersection leaned his head out his car window and yelled, "Go back to your own f*cking neighborhood!" I was afraid at the time and later angry. But as I look back now, I can understand why the people stared and why the kid blocked the sidewalk and why the man yelled out his window.

I know the motives of the people in my group were genuine. It was a bold move to leave the comfortable and to take that walk. And of course it is not wrong to seek to pray for someone. But I think of how this was perceived. As we walked through that neighborhood, the people didn't know what we were doing, and neither did we. We didn't know the man in the car—his life, his story, what it was like to grow up in his neighborhood. We were going to climb into our bus with cushy seats and a DVD player and probably never come back. We didn't know him, so we didn't know what to pray for—how could we? We hadn't really earned the right to step into that situation.

We didn't know our neighbors, so we couldn't offer anything relevant to their lives. At times in our history, the church has become so far removed that it has literally allowed its neighbors to die at its doorstep.

During Hitler's reign in Germany, much of the church became irrelevant. Hitler was reported to have said of Christians, "You can do anything you want with them. They will submit ... they are insignificant little people, submissive as dogs." Under persecution from Hitler, many in the church became loyal to him, becoming members of what became known as the Reich Church. Dietrich Bonhoeffer, one of the few Christians who resisted Hitler, felt that much of the reason the church fell to this was because of a belief in what he called "cheap grace." They had come to believe in a gospel that did not require action.[1] So the church found itself standing in the midst of a hell storm and getting swept away in it. Millions of neighbors were gassed or burned and much of the church did nothing. If I place myself in that context I really don't know if I would have possessed the courage to follow Bonhoeffer. Yet I believe the decision not to would have been to forfeit the purpose of Christianity.

Without a purpose, Christianity becomes irrelevant. It is trite to hand out a Christian tract to someone enduring a divorce or drinking down chemicals to kill their cancer if we have nothing to back up the words on that paper. It is useless to talk about life if we have nothing to offer those dying around us. Death is so overwhelming that people are looking for more than a vague promise or a shallow invitation to come to Jesus. Death still reigns and runs loose. This leaves people to conclude either that God isn't real or that he can't help.

CHAPTER 10

JACK FELL DOWN

Many look at death and decide God either doesn't exist or can't help.

When we consider the death around us, so much of it seems random and pointless. People have trouble believing in a God that is both good and powerful, because this type of God does not fit into the picture of our suffering. For some the easiest answer is that God does not exist. Others still cling to the notion of a deity, but he is either too cruel to care or too weak to act.

I walked into a room to get a glass of water, and the TV was turned to CNN. I saw a flood in Missouri burying a town. Statues with heads tilted toward heaven looked like drowning victims lifting their chins for a last breath of air. As the reporters discussed the flooding, a message bar scrolled across the bottom of the screen. From this I learned of a gunman who had killed a defense official, a suicide bomber who had killed six, and a suspected drone attack that had killed ten. And this was not a unique day of news. Not long after this, the same reporters told me about female infants who were being killed in Pakistan because they were the wrong gender.

There are so many deaths that simply feel unjust. There was a pastor at the church I grew up in who lost a baby not long after the child was born. I always felt like she wore sadness. And I remember my parents once pointing out the gravestone of a baby who had died. It was a very small stone, adorned with angels. I knew two boys who lost their father. The family knew for a long time that he was going to die, but I recall seeing them after he'd gone. The boys just stood together with their mom and stared at the dead grass. There was nothing else to do but stand. And my mom's dad died when she was ten. The degree and nature of this type of loss surpasses grief. A young child is not meant to lose a parent, and parents are not meant to bury their children in small graves. The emotions that accompany this scope of loss can't even be defined, because it is not just the loss of a life; it is the sense of something deeply out of line and massively hopeless. It feels as though there is some vast evil set against us.

We look at this, and our suffering often feels random and pointless. Is there a reason? Is there a cause for all of this? Some would answer no, there is no cause, there is no one to blame, there is no point—because for them, there is no God.

Friedrich Nietzsche said that God is dead. He followed atheism all the way to the end of the damp tunnel and grabbed at a true understanding of what it means. Atheism means no God. Without God, nature becomes the source of all things. Nature is blind and cold and indifferent. It knows nothing of good and evil. If a tsunami destroys a coastline, it is tragic and devastating, but no one accuses nature of being evil. There was no reason for the wall of water that smashed a city and swallowed the dead. It just happened. In this context, suffering becomes pointless and random.

Nature is random, but the randomness is supposed to be curbed by natural selection. The "force" of natural selection is said to steer us on toward the prize; the prize being survival and evolutionary progress. The goal in the game of evolution is to survive and make lots of babies. Nature will reward or punish based on the behavior of a species or individual. The "right behaviors" are the ones that help a species survive. The "wrong" behaviors are the ones that hinder survival.

This seems simple enough until we consider the implications. The one who truly believes God does not exist cannot condemn terrorism or rape or child trafficking or genocide. They cannot condemn these actions because nature allows, and may even reward, these behaviors. Exploiting, enslaving, and killing can all assist certain groups in gaining dominance over other groups, thus ensuring their survival. As a result, many of the actions that are traditionally labeled as evil could be considered perfectly acceptable in a world without God. It is a bloody brawl for survival. So violence toward the competition could be very "right" and mercy toward the competition could prove to be fatally "wrong." This creates a conflict within many people though. It is hard to get the head and the heart to agree on this matter.

In the book *Jesus Among Other Gods*, Ravi Zacharias told about a conversation he had with some atheist students at Oxford. He asked how the students would feel if he were to cut up a baby in front of them. Would this be wrong? After thinking for some time, a student said, "I would not like it, but no, I could not say you have done anything wrong."[1] This young man was conflicted between his mental position and the reality of his heart.

Charles Darwin demonstrated a similar angst that came from trying to maintain his atheism (which was required by his theory) and his morality (which was required by his conscience). Darwin was repelled by the concept of slavery and yet he realized that slavery allowed certain groups to thrive and advance. It worked very neatly within his theory that the fittest will survive. Benjamin Wiker described this irony well in his biography of Darwin.

> Darwin's theory, which he believed in with all the passion of a religion, which he cared for with all the fierce tenderness of a father for his beloved child, contradicted Darwin's own most sincere humanity, his hatred of slavery, his native abhorrence at seeing anyone or anything suffer, his almost epic kindness and gentleness with his family, friends, servants, neighbors and strangers.[2]

The result of all this is that people are reduced to mere animals and no one is really accountable for anything. In order to be held accountable, there must be some higher authority that we report to. But under atheism, there is no such authority. I read the following message on the American Atheist website: "So if Adam and Eve and the Talking Snake are myths, the Original Sin is also a myth, right? … No Adam and Eve means no need for a savior."[3] Again, atheism suggests that evil is not real and no one is really to blame for suffering.

While it is true that many people think this way, it does not appear that many people actually feel this way. We don't act like no one is to blame. We don't act like there is no good and evil. After a bomb ripped through the federal building in Oklahoma, leaving a gnarled mess of steel and concrete and killing both adults and children, people sat in the quiet presence of a very tangible evil. People wanted to find the man to blame. We put criminals on trial and then place them in small rooms with a toilet and a mattress. Or sometimes we go further and put a needle in their arm.

On one hand, atheism seems to explain why this massive ship is sinking—there is no captain in control. Only the blind, fierce wind of nature directs our course. But atheism does not explain why we still want to speak of right and wrong, and why we still recognize the presence of evil in the world. This seemingly innate moral sense of good and evil has led many people to believe there must be a source of our convictions and therefore there must be a God.

Unlike atheism, most religions hold human beings accountable for the suffering we see. The common theme is that the suffering we encounter is the direct result of our folly.

Hinduism teaches reincarnation, which is the belief that the human soul, once it dies, will enter a new womb and be born again. The womb you enter with each new birth hinges entirely on your conduct in the previous life. The following verse explains this process.

> Accordingly, those who are of pleasant conduct here—
> the prospect is, indeed, that they will enter a pleasant womb ... But those who are of stinking conduct here—
> the prospect is, indeed, that they will enter a stinking womb of a dog, or the womb of a swine, or the womb of an outcast.[4]

Buddhism holds a similar teaching. Buddha said, "Whatever actions I do, good or bad, I shall become their heir."[5] With both Hinduism and Buddhism, our present pain is actually the punishment for our sins in previous life. The Abrahamic religions also make a connection between human actions and suffering.

Within Islam, one is responsible for one's actions and must hope to obtain mercy from Allah to avoid pain. The individual can increase the chances of receiving such mercy by undertaking enough good deeds. Sumbul Ali-Karamali, a student of Islam, told a childhood story of a prostitute who brought water to a dog dying of thirst. She explained the prostitute was destined for heaven because of her kindness. She wrote, "Islam allows people to go to heaven if they have undertaken enough good works, even if they are not perfect, even if they are not Muslim."[6]

Similar ideas can be found within Judaism. The rabbis (teachers within Judaism) held to the concept that there are two impulses in every person: the good impulse, yetzer ha-tov, and the evil impulse, yetzer ha-ra. So people have within them the capacity for good or evil.[7] Abraham Cohen, author of Everyman's Talmud, describes this phenomenon as "two urges—one to evil and the other to goodness." He also says that "the character of a person is determined by which of the two impulses is dominant within him."[8] These impulses then lead to actual consequences in life. Suffering and joy are tied up in this.

The general sense in all of these religions is if you are good, good things will happen. If you are bad, bad things will happen. But often, in reality, it seems messier than that. There are things that happen to people that feel deeply unjust, either because the recipient of suffering strikes us as someone truly innocent, like an infant child, or because the degree of suffering seems way out of proportion for any one person to take on. This is where things begin to get very complicated.

The Jewish scriptures contain a story about a man named Job. Job is presented as a righteous man. The story even portrays God supporting this claim. And then calamity falls on Job like acid rain. His oxen, donkeys, and camels are stolen and his servants massacred; his sheep are burned up in a falling flame; his house collapses when a strong wind blows out the four corners; and his sons and daughters are crushed. Finally he develops painful soars from the top of his head to the souls of his feet. So standing or lying down, he is in anguish.

His wife tells him to curse God and die. Then his friends show up to offer help, but they end up arguing philosophy. The conversation amounts to the friends trying to figure out what Job had done to bring on such hell. In other words, the suffering must have come because of Job's sin. Job denies any wrongdoing and cries to God for an answer.

So what do we do with Job? What do we do when the good-versus-bad formula fails to explain things? Not only do we see what feels like a distorted amount of suffering, but there are those whom many of us would label as "bad" who seem to be getting along fine: no sores, no dead children, no welfare checks. It is at this point that many come to the conclusion that God either can't help or won't help. God is either powerful or loving—but not both.

The powerful God could end our pain but chooses not to. Some feel he may arrange for our suffering. It reminds me of something Heather and I saw when we lived in Virginia. We were walking and found a nylon rope hanging from a tree branch. The rope had big knots tied in it. It was like a rope swing except it was too short and too high off the ground, and there was no water around. The rope, we found out, was used to train dogs to fight. They would be lifted up to the rope, instructed to hold on to it with their teeth, and left to dangle until their jaws couldn't hold any longer. This is one explanation for a universe in which God and evil coexist. Some see God organizing dog fights from the balcony of heaven.

On the other hand, the loving God has a heart for people, but his hands are bound behind his back. Evil was somehow unleashed, and it now exists beyond his control. God is a friend who cries at our pain. He will listen on the phone. But he does not have the authority to stop hell from rolling over us. Of the two, the loving God feels easier to accept. At least he is nice—even if he is powerless. Though the favorite, he is simply the lesser of two evils, and we are still stuck in death.

But there is one other possible explanation for God in light of human suffering and death. This explanation is unique to Christianity.

Christianity also suggests there is a battle waging within us between good and evil. And Christianity strongly holds that suffering is the consequence of human sin. In this sense it agrees with the other religions of the world. But there is an important difference that renders Christianity unique. Within Christianity, it is not a question of good *or* bad. It is a matter of good *and* bad.

Creation was good. God said it repeatedly. And people are unique among creation in that we were actually created in the image of God. So this was the status of humanity—good. But in various places in the Bible we learn otherwise. In the Old Testament, one writer stated, "All have turned away, all have become corrupt; there is no one who does good, not even one."[9] The apostle Paul echoed this in his letter to the Roman church, saying that all fall short of the glory of God.[10] And Jesus said no one is good except for God.[11] Why the apparent contradiction? What happened? The answer is that there was a tragic incident that took place and continues to replay every second, including this one. Humanity fell.

You may have anticipated that answer. You know the story. Two naked people communicate with a snake and eat an apple. Then God gets angry. We already saw the story recapped on the American Atheist website.

But the Christian idea of the fall is far more serious than anything evoked by a simple retelling of Adam and Eve. The act the humanity has been engaging in since near the beginning is not an act of chewing on fruit. The crime committed by humanity illustrated in the Genesis story is not just disobedience to an arbitrary rule. It is an act of adultery and even treason.

The Christian view is that God gave life and gave himself to humanity. The first people actually went on walks through the woods with the eternal God. They were made for a relationship, tied firmly to God, who literally breathed the air that caused their lungs to swell. And the command from God to leave one tree untouched was, among other things, an exercise in trust. Would humanity hang on to the life offered by their God? Humanity did not. We mistrusted the heart of God. We chose another lover. And we also determined ourselves to be more capable of securing life, so we gave ourselves a promotion. In an act of mutiny we made ourselves kings and queens of our own universe.

And the result was a divorce. I've worked many different jobs, and in one of those jobs I frequently came in contact with divorce documents. These documents generally provided some sort of explanation in the first paragraph—an explanation for why the marriage had dissolved. The language was basically consistent every time. The court had determined that the two people once bound together in heart and spirit had experienced an irreversible breakdown due to irreconcilable differences.

When humanity fell, its relationship to the life-giving God was severed. At this point death entered. Humanity willingly rejected the life of God and chose death. Freedom to choose was given, because love demands it. A love that is mandated is not love. A child in chains is not a true child. This left the option for rebellion, and humanity chose it.

And in this act, a heavy door was kicked in. This is the other reason the theft from the tree of knowledge was so severe. It knocked something loose in the universe. Evil entered and unimaginable sin would follow. The first children would discover how to murder one another, and it deteriorated from there. When humanity fell, it was as though we grabbed onto the corner of the universe and dragged it down with us as we slid into a hole. We didn't just break our crowns, we broke the pail and the water and the hill. Death now covers everything.

While Christianity teaches death is the result of human sin, there is another element to human suffering. In the story of the fall, there is another key character that must be addressed. Suffering cannot be understood without acknowledging the existence of an evil force that is distinct from humanity. I am referring to the Devil. In talking about Satan, I should state that Christians seem to treat this topic with different degrees of urgency. Some obsess about it, blaming everything on the Devil. Others live like evil is fake and no threat exists.

The evil figure in the story of the fall is very subtle, so it is easy to ignore. He didn't bite the woman, driving venom into her fresh veins. He just told the two people that God was wrong and that there was more for them.[12] He quietly led them away from the source of their life, tempting them into a willing rejection of God. It seems minor, but the intended result was to lead them into death. There was premeditation to bring a fatal consequence. And the threat continues, though it is unseen.

My wife showed me an article about radiation from cell phones, cordless phones, and baby monitors. The idea was that we should try to keep a distance from these devices while using them and that we are basically surrounded by these waves of radiation all the time. Now, every time I use a cell phone I picture this green smoke pouring out of the speakers creeping into my nostrils or wrapping itself around me like a vine. This is a good picture for Satan. He is an invisible menace. Paul said that our struggle is not against flesh and blood, but against the powers of this dark world and against spiritual forces of evil.[13] Why do we see acts of evil that can hardly be spoken of? Why is there such fierce brutality? This is not an attempt to excuse sin. But the truth is, there is something set against us, something that desires our death. The Devil is eternally engaged in tempting us and deceiving us into being used as instruments of suffering. Jesus called the Devil a thief who came to steal, kill, and destroy.[14] Aren't we surrounded by theft and murder and destruction?

But this brings us to another question. Humanity chose sin and opened a window to allow in this tear gas. The Devil is real, and he harbors homicidal intentions toward humanity. So this is how Christianity explains the cause of our suffering. But even if God is not the source of human suffering, why doesn't he intervene more? Love demanded freedom, but it also demands action, doesn't it? If God could stop it and he really loves us, why doesn't he? He wouldn't have to swat every mosquito that lands on the back of our necks, just the ones carrying malaria.

If God didn't act, it would be hard to suggest that Christianity is relevant. Even if we don't deserve his salvation, we need it. But what if God has acted and we just didn't realize it?

CHAPTER 11

KILLED BUT NOT DEAD

Christianity is a relevant religion.

This seems like an odd statement, because we have seen a Christianity that often does little to address the death we encounter. Beyond that, we know that Jesus was executed. And we have to ask—if he has the strength to remove death, why did his story involve such an abrupt ending? It doesn't sound like the story of a conquering general. The savior was slain. His efforts to save seem noble—he gave up his life. But this act is supposed to have ended our death. Yet it is still around, lingering like a foul odor. Christians claim that God has acted to save us. But we don't feel saved. How do we explain this?

Awhile back I was reading a book by Lee Strobel. He was also after an explanation for suffering. He interviewed this priest who had many good things to say. But the one that stayed with me was an analogy of a hunter, a bear, and a steel trap. In his story, the bear was caught in this trap, and the hunter was trying to free him but couldn't communicate this.[1] The story was good, but I was having trouble relating to the bear. This was probably because I'm not a bear, so I don't know much about how they interpret suffering. The part of the story that stayed with me was the steel trap. I kept thinking about it, and this picture came to me about our situation. I've shaped it into a short story, and I'd like to share it with you.

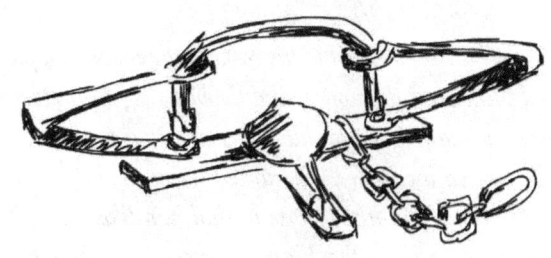

THE TRAP

There was a boy who lived with his father outside of town. Their property was heavily wooded. The boy only came inside to sleep. He loved the woods. When he grew older, his father allowed him to go beyond the property line but warned against traveling too far. Beyond a certain point, the coyote population was heavy. His father set traps in this area of the woods as a measure against the predators.

There was another man who lived deep in these woods—a hermit. The boy had only seen him in town a few times, once at the hardware store buying a box of nails, and another time at the café, sitting alone at the corner table eating a piece of pie.

One day, when the boy was deep in the woods, he saw the hermit chopping down a tree. The man looked up and noticed him. Then he coughed, spit, and went back to chopping. The boy called out, "Why do you live out here?"

"Out here, I'm a king," he said, still chopping. The boy thought maybe he was crazy. But something pulled at him.

"Aren't you afraid of the coyotes?"

The man stopped and turned to the boy. "What coyotes?" he said. Then he started to laugh. His laughter hit the trees and rolled over the leaves.

The boy turned and walked away. His ears were hot. He was embarrassed and then angry. He began to wonder if his father had made up the coyotes to prevent him from finding whatever was out there. So the next day, he decided to find out. He reached the point his father had marked with an old rag tied to a tree branch. He ripped the rag from the branch, threw it on the ground, and kept walking. The boy felt a surge of freedom. He began to run. But suddenly he heard the sound of snapping metal and was slammed to the ground. He felt a pain sear through his leg, and then he passed out.

When he awoke, he was frantic with fear. He didn't remember what had happened. Then he noticed that the leaves around him were sticky and red. He looked down and saw the steel trap embedded in his calf. He threw up and passed out again. The sun came and went more than once, and the boy's leg began to grow numb. He sat in a daze, sometimes calling out for his father and sometimes cursing him. Then, one day, he heard steps in the leaves. He turned to see the hermit walking toward him. There was an animal following close behind him like a pet. It was a coyote.

"What happened to you?" the hermit asked. The boy was afraid and

didn't answer.

The old man pulled a bottle of whiskey out of his pocket. He kicked his head back and swallowed some of the liquid. It dribbled down his chin and hung from his beard in a string. Then he bent down and splashed the whiskey on the boy's leg. At first, the boy screamed as the liquor burned his open wounds. But then his leg went numb again. And for the first time, the constant ache left him.

The hermit set the bottle on the ground next to the boy and walked back into the woods. The boy's lips were caked in dried blood, cracked and thirsty. He grabbed the bottle and began to drink. For about a day, he felt happy in a drunken stupor.

But the alcohol wore off, and the pain in his leg began to pulse again, as if the jaws of the steel trap were releasing and then clamping back down, over and over. The pain had almost overtaken the boy when he saw a figure running toward him. This time it was his father. The boy's father reached him and grabbed him, kissing his head. Then, he began to tear back the fabric of his son's pants around the area of the wound. The fabric had fused itself to the boy's skin, and he cried out, "Get away from me!"

The father looked at his son with wet eyes and said, "I am going to free you."

The boy cried out again as his father continued to clear the area of the wound. "Just go get me some more whiskey," the boy said. But the father ignored his son's demand and kept working.

The release mechanism on the trap was broken, so the father began to pry open the jaws of the trap with his hands. As the metal teeth tore loose from the boy's skin, he felt the pain of the initial accident all over again—as though he were living it in reverse. With his free leg, he tried to kick his father away. He was in shock, and in his confusion he thought his father was inflicting the pain.

When his father had opened the trap far enough, he wedged his own shoulder between the jaws to hold it while he freed his son. Then his father pulled free of the trap, blood pouring from his hands and his shoulder blade near his neck, and he carried his son out of the woods.

He loaded the boy into their truck and drove three hours to the hospital. Once the father saw that the boy was being attended to by paramedics, he leaned forward into the steering wheel, closed his eyes, and died.

So why doesn't God intervene to end our suffering? The claim of Christianity is that he has. We think of suffering as hail hurled from heaven. Each painful event is an isolated pellet, and we are standing under these pellets, collecting dents. But I don't believe this is a suitable picture of our suffering. We are not being hit by balls of ice—we have fallen through the ice, and it has frozen around us. We are trapped.

Suffering is the essence of our existence. We have been immersed in it from birth. It is our reality. We need freedom. But this process of being freed is painful. It has to be because of our condition. We are locked in the mouth of this trap, and when God comes to initiate our healing, he is going to pull the spikes apart. And it is going to hurt. We, like the boy, misunderstand our condition. The pulse of pain feels like punishment from the Father when actually it is the evidence that he has come to free us.

The way we misinterpret our suffering reminds me of the year I spent teaching fourth grade. Oceanview Elementary School was an old bomb-shelter-like building—walls of concrete three feet thick and giant windows with old, foggy glass. The ceilings felt fifteen feet high. In the lobby, there was a picture of the first class of students standing in a circle around a tree. All of the students were white. This was Virginia, so when this school was first built, schools were likely still segregated. The demographics had changed since then—but a subtle tension hovered (or at least I felt like it did). I was going to storm into that school and change the lives of every ten-year-old kid who walked through the door.

Instead, I ran into fierce resistance. Most of the year I felt like the kids didn't understand my intentions. I wanted good for them. But my efforts were often not received in this way. The easiest way to illustrate what I am saying would be to show you a drawing one of my students created one day instead of working on her math lesson.

KILLED BUT NOT DEAD

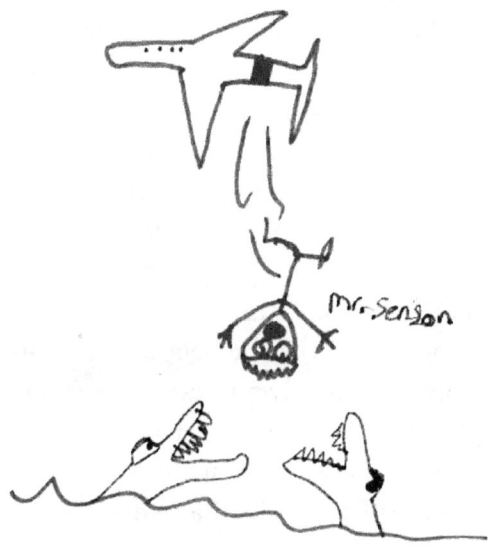

God has come for us but we don't see it. Perhaps part of the reason we don't see it is because we have trouble making a connection between Jesus' execution and our situation. In the story, the freedom offered by the father was tangible. There was a clear connection between the father's death and the son's life. But our reality is more abstract. Our trap is invisible. How does all of this actually work? How did this God "come for us" to "free us"? If we can't take this story and actually apply it to life, then it can't be very relevant. Therefore, we need to see how it applies.

We are told that Jesus died to give us life. The prophet Isaiah, speaking of the Savior who would come, said that by his wounds we were healed.[2] And as we consider the accounts of Jesus' death, it seems as though he was very intentional about the importance of this event.

Repeatedly Jesus warned his friends he was going to have to die. His mission was about life, but it was also about his death. There is a beautiful story near the end where a woman poured oil on Jesus' feet and washed them with her hair. It was an act of humble sacrifice. Scrubbing dirt away not with a rag, but with herself. Jesus indicated that it was also preparation for his burial.³

The writers of the Gospels tell of a scene where Jesus prayed the night before his execution. He asked God to provide another way.⁴ There was tension and passion in this prayer. The blood vessels in his skin seemed to break and stain his sweat. We don't hear God's response to Jesus. But he was arrested shortly after this prayer and he did not resist. Peter actually took out a blade and severed the ear of one of the men in the mob. But Jesus told Peter to lower the sword, and then he healed the man.⁵ This was not an hour of weakness. It was a definitive choice. It was like he believed his death was absolutely vital to the mission—like his dying and our living were irrevocably bound together. So how do we make sense of this?

I think the answer to this is found in a story John told in his Gospel. Jesus was talking to his friend Martha, whose brother Lazarus had died. Martha was troubled because Jesus hadn't come earlier. But Jesus comforted her saying, "Your brother will rise again."

To this Martha said, "I know he will rise again in the resurrection at the last day."

Then Jesus responded, "I am the resurrection and the life. The one who believes in me will live, even though they die; and whoever lives by believing in me will never die."⁶

This seems odd, because it should be one or the other. Either we are alive or we are dead. Maybe Jesus was just saying he could raise people from the dead. Or maybe he was saying something else. I think Jesus was trying to tell Martha that there is more than one kind of death.

Think with me for a moment about a wake you have been to. You walk up, and there is a body lying in a box. It is the person you knew—kind of. Her eyelids are pulled shut, her hands are crossed on her stomach, and so on. But at the same time, you know the person isn't there. She is somewhere else. The body is there, but this other part of her isn't. And this other part is really the more important part. It is the part you knew and talked to and loved. And though it was obviously attached to the body before, it is clearly independent from the body because it is not there now. It is like there are these two parts to us: body and everything that is not body. We usually call this other part our spirit. We can see these parts are distinct when we stand holding a glass of red punch in a funeral home. And we hope that even though the body has died, the spirit still lives.

But there are other times we see dead people who are not in a casket. They are walking around and talking and buying things and living, and yet they don't seem alive. Or perhaps this is you. You have already swallowed food today and you drank a glass of water and your body is working, but you feel dead. I have felt this in very real ways before. And I can't help but think that in the same way my body can die, so can my spirit. We can see the results of spiritual death all around us, but we don't understand it in those terms. In other words, we don't usually realize what is actually killing us from the inside out. We feel it, but we are not aware of what is happening. So how could God communicate this to us?

I believe God carries out acts in the physical world in order to show us what was happening in the spiritual world. One thing we do understand is what it means to save a life. Take Dorwan Stoddard, for example. This man was at the grocery store with his wife when Jared Loughner started shooting people. Stoddard jumped on top of his wife and took three bullets in the back. She lived. He didn't.[7] We understand on a deep level the power of one surrendering his body to preserve another life. And the impact is even greater when the hero could have avoided death.

The greatest stories turn on this same idea. Even if they are fictional we know they are somehow true. One of my favorite movies is *Stranger Than Fiction* with Will Ferrell. Ferrell's character, Harold Crick, begins hearing a voice, which turns out to be that of the narrator. The plot gets a bit confusing because he seems to be the main character in a novel being written, and yet he is also a real person. Toward the end of the movie, Harold finds the author just as she is about to kill off his character—which he thinks will actually kill him. Initially he begs for a rewrite, but after reading the manuscript and learning how the story is going to end, Harold tells the writer to finish her work. He wants her to write it even though it may kill him. The next morning, he willingly steps in front of a bus to save a boy's life.

Jesus' execution on the cross was God communicating something to us in way we could understand. Something was taking place on a far greater level. In the unseen world, there is an unseen battle raging around us, and our souls are dying. And in this unseen, spiritual reality, Jesus took a bullet in the back, jumped in front of a bus, and wedged himself into the jaws of a steel trap. The fact that God came to free us does not suggest that our crime was petty; it suggests that his love is deep. God illustrated this saving act in the unseen world, through the tangible death of Jesus in a physical body. This is why his death was required and why nothing could stop him from stepping into that death. And the story doesn't end there. If our spirits can actually die now while our physical bodies are still alive, perhaps they can be resurrected as well.

It was not just that God was trying to prevent our spiritual death. He also wants to actually restore our lives and even give us new life. Jesus surrendered his body to the bony arms of death to communicate the saving of our souls. Then his body was resurrected to communicate the restoration of our souls.

Jesus said that we could be born a second time—as though the death can be erased and we can be made again, anew.[8] He also said he could restore our spirits and actually place his Spirit in us.[9] The same Spirit that empowered him to live such a beautiful life can live in us.[10] It is as though God is burying a pacemaker in our chest that will propel our hearts forward. And since God is eternal, his Spirit does not burn out. So if we receive his Spirit, it will last forever. The lives we are getting in exchange for our old lives will be eternal. Maybe this is what Jesus meant when he said that even if we die we will live.

And as we turn to take up his salvation, God asks us to sign a release form. We must give our lives over to this God and give him permission to cut us open. This surgery is required to remove the decay. There will likely be pain involved in the process of being remade. And rehab will be required as well, because Jesus wants to teach us how to walk again. We need to learn how to walk, because we are not being invited to sit and wait.

We are being invited to follow.

CHAPTER 12

THE FOG BURNED UP

The purpose of Christianity is to follow Jesus.

The church is not meant to wait comfortably for Jesus' return. The church is meant to move and spread. Christianity quickly becomes irrelevant when the church sits still. When Jesus left, we are told, he poured out his Spirit. He intends for his followers to behave like a body that can receive his Spirit and take action in the world.

Some hear this call to action and interpret it as an instruction to just do more for God. I don't believe that this is what Jesus meant. So before we can look at what it means to follow Jesus, we need to look at what it doesn't mean.

The salvation of the world is not up to us. Any who suggest this are aligning themselves with something other than Christianity.

Islamic writer Ziauddin Sardar wrote, "The way to paradise is to live a selfless, spiritual life devoted to good deeds," and also, "This is why belief alone is not good enough; it has to be supplemented with good, just and charitable deeds. The account that one has to render on the Day of Judgment is a personal account—only one's own deeds, and not intercession by someone else, will lead to salvation."[1]

For reformed Jews, the belief is every individual must "live as if he or she, individually, has the responsibility to bring about the messianic age." Author David Ariel says that "Reform Judaism rejected the traditional Jewish messianism." It removed from the prayer book all references to the Messiah and to an eventual return to Israel. The Reform concept of messianism has come to mean the result of human effort on behalf of creating the perfect world.[2]

Even those who do not adhere to a religion can take it upon themselves to save the world. Some seek to restore the atmosphere and protect the polar ice caps from decay. Others seek to save the nation by campaigning for the candidate they think will usher in a new era.

There are even some who have set out to eliminate religion, believing this will allow peace to rain down and soak the earth.

But the truth is, none of us are fit to save. The psalmist wrote, "Who can live and not see death, or who can escape the power of the grave?"[3] And G. K. Chesterton said this of the one who would claim the ability to save humanity: "So you are the Creator and Redeemer of the world: but what a small world it must be! What a little heaven you must inhabit, with angels not bigger than butterflies!"[4]

It should be evident from our own lives that we cannot eternally save ourselves let alone anyone else. And this is not the call of Christianity. Christianity starts with the promise of salvation. The Messiah has already come. Jesus agitated the priests in Jerusalem and undermined the kings of Israel. He disassembled the machines built to oppress the weak and guard those in power. He removed sickness and destroyed death. He kicked a hole in the door of hell and pushed ajar the door of heaven. But this is not a call to lie down and do nothing.

Jesus destroyed death and secured salvation. But then Jesus left the kingdom in the hands of his followers. He didn't leave them alone—he sent power from heaven—but he ultimately entrusted the advancement of his kingdom to the church that would assemble in his name.

Jesus brought the kingdom of heaven, but the kingdom of hell is still real. There is a war to be fought for people's lives—not a war fought with steel and smoke, but an unseen war that can only be won with ridiculous and near-impossible acts of love. To become a Christian is to enlist in a war against hell and suffering. Jesus intended his church to be relevant and for his followers to get messy in their efforts to love—not because we can save anyone, but because we've been saved and can point others to this salvation.

So what does it look like to follow Jesus? The reality is that it would feel much easier to follow Jesus if we could see him. How do you follow an invisible man? When Jesus was in a body, one could choose to first watch where he was going and then go to that place with him. But what does it look like now?

There was a rich young man who approached Jesus and asked what it would take to follow him. Jesus told him to keep the commandments, which the man had done. Then Jesus told him he should sell everything he had and give the money to the destitute. Then he could follow him. The man quietly left Jesus' presence. Many read this story and determine that the way to follow Jesus is to sell all of their possessions to feed the poor.

Then there was the woman who broke open the bottle of expensive perfume and poured it out over Jesus feet. Jesus' students wanted to rebuke the woman for wasting the jar. It could have been sold and the proceeds could have then been given to the poor. In this case, Jesus praised the woman for her choice. He stated her story would be told to the nations. Some will read this and conclude the way to follow Jesus is to sit at his feet in worship.

And perhaps both are true. But I still need more. If I am going to give up possessions to follow him, I still need to know where he is going. If am going to worship at his feet, I need to know where he resides.

So where are the places Jesus is going? Where is the place he resides? Among the suffering, where else? The bleeding, the addicted, the terrified, the freezing, the heartbroken, the malnourished—to these we must go. And if the church is operating as it should, then in the times we are cold or hungry or afraid, others will be coming for us. The goal out in this desolate middle between Jesus' first coming and his return is not to escape suffering. That is not actually possible anyway. The goal is to love each other so well that we can endure and even overcome suffering. Then our suffering will not be wasted. Instead, it will accomplish something beautiful in us that would not otherwise be possible. Then death will begin to die—and we will begin to actually live.

When we go where Jesus would go, we will find him there. His body will actually appear and take shape around his Spirit. Muscles will be woven together over bone, and legs will lift feet over the ground. We will see his body because we will become his body—the church. And each member of this body has a distinct assignment. Ask yourself what makes you come alive. What do you desire? From where do you derive your deepest joy? These things will reveal to you your place in the body. As you live out this function, you will contribute to the common purpose of the body as a whole, which is to bring life to a dying world.

This kind of church would be relevant in the world. And while I am still trying to learn what it looks like in my life, I have seen many examples of the body at work.

When I met Heather at a Bible camp, she was terrified to counsel young girls. She'd been to camp once as a young girl, and the counselor had communicated a misguided message about beauty. Doubt filled her as to whether she could teach. But she believed Jesus was leading her to this camp, and so she followed him. And that summer, she sat in a platform tent and taught teenage girls that they were beautiful. She helped to remove the diluted version of beauty many of them had choked on their whole lives.

In Minneapolis, my sister worked with a program that placed homeless young adults with families. Many of these kids had been evicted by their own parents. There were churches coming together to form a body, and there were kids finding homes.

There is a program called *Youth with a Mission* that prepares people to integrate into places like Cambodia and Nepal. My brother found himself riding an old bike through a country filled with mostly young people. The old had been eliminated during a season of slaughter. He worked late hours in a restaurant and taught biology to a few kids by the light of a cell phone. He found God in the small children he met, and they saw Jesus in him.

There is a pastor who lives on a reservation in South Dakota. When I met him, about eight to ten people showed up for his Sunday service—mostly for the free lunch that followed. But he stayed. He played kickball with lost kids and loved a group that had been dishonored and robbed of hope.

Another pastor I met once took a shovel over to his neighbor's house and helped him clear the snow from his driveway. The neighbor had a Confederate flag hanging in his garage, and this pastor was African American.

My youth pastor took time to counsel me—a young junior high kid battling demons of lust. He prepared me to love my future wife with integrity and purity.

And then there was Dietrich Bonhoeffer. Though most of the German church folded under Hitler, there was a small cell that refused to die. The Confessing Church was lead by Bonhoeffer. He preached against the violent reign of Hitler, and he rejoiced even after being imprisoned for his resistance. Before he was taken to the gallows, he held a little church service. In closing the service (and his life), he read First Peter 1:3: "Blessed be the God and Father of our Lord Jesus Christ, which according to his abundant mercy hath begotten us again unto a lively hope by the resurrection of Jesus Christ from the dead."[5]

Sometimes there are giant, broad movements in the church. Other times, it spreads underground through these quiet actions, these tiny movements, these thankless jobs. And it isn't always beautiful or clean. Usually it is messy, and though we all need help, we resist it because of our brokenness. We've been wounded so long we flail our legs and kick when the Father comes to free us from our traps or sends someone else as the representation of his body and as a minister of healing. But it is in this way that the church becomes relevant—small people following Jesus to the places he is going and carrying his life to chase out death.

This journey of learning to follow Jesus reminds me of the morning I went to work without sleeping. I had stayed up until four in the morning finishing the first draft of this book. I then got up at six to go to my day job. The drive to work was blurry. There was fog hanging above the road, and there was a mist of rain, like it was coming from a giant spray bottle. My eyes also had a fog in them. It was like I was wearing dirty contacts. The windshield wipers just smeared the fog on the glass, and my fingers smeared the fog in my eyes. I couldn't tell where one fog ended and the other fog started. The only thing I could really see in any of this was little red lights moving on the road and little gold lights overhead. The small lights were random and fuzzy, like dying light bulbs coated in dust.

Most of my life felt like that fog. Confused and lost, I was spinning my head around looking for something. There were little lights teasing me everywhere but nothing solid to hang onto. But now a brighter light has come over the hill. I could see it even before it reached the top. The trees were illuminated, and a glow began to rise on the road. And then I saw the source of that light come into view. A man named Jesus leaned out the window of a truck as he slowly passed and invited me to follow him.

So I made a U-turn. And it is not just that he is pouring light in and cutting through the fog; he is actually going somewhere. I believe he knows the way out of the darkness, and so following him is more than just seeing; it is realizing that hope is real. And as we drive, there are times when the fog thins out enough to see the place where we are going. Light moves through the gaps in the trees and sprays the road. At other times the fog is heavy and suffocating. And I swear I can hear the whispers of some dark voice pouring out of the fog telling me I will never find the way. But I believe one day those voices will be silenced and the fog will all dry up and we will arrive at the top of a hill that looks over the place we'd been moving toward all along. And God will be there. And the fog won't survive, because the light will be too strong.

And the thing is, I don't just want to find a way out of the fog for myself. We are not to follow Jesus with tunnel vision. I've got my family in the car with me. We've got the hazard lights for anyone else feeling lost as they drive through this fog. And there are cars with broken fan belts and cars that have rolled into ditches, and we are called to stop and get out—to feel the fog press against our faces as we try to help. We offer the only hope we have, which is to follow the man who not only knows the way out, but who also cleared the road.

At the end of the road we will climb to the top of that hill, and the fog will fade into nothing. And I hope we will look back and see a train of cars behind us.

AFTERWORD

You may have arrived at the end of this book with a question. If Christianity is not intolerant, irrational, or irrelevant, why do so many Christians display these traits? Why don't more followers of this religion reflect that which is true about it?

That is a good question. And the answer is simple. Christianity is impossible—almost.

It is way easier to drift toward extreme aggression or extreme apathy. But Jesus asks his followers to exist in this place of tension between restraint and action. He asks us to act in a way that is the opposite of what feels normal. The kingdom he established is vastly different than any kingdom on earth. It is a kingdom where anger equals murder, and yet the repentant murderer receives amnesty. It is a kingdom where wise men are considered fools and little children have access to the knowledge of heaven. And it is a kingdom where one must die in order to live.

Love your enemy, become like a little child, take up your cross—these are the things Jesus asks of those of us who would follow him. And without his Spirit, these things are not possible. It is like walking out on a swinging bridge that could snap at any time. From either side of the ravine extremists are firing bullets into the air. Not to mention the fact that there is a real spiritual enemy providing the ammunition. There is a fierce power set against those who would seek to follow this Jesus.

Those crossing this bridge should not be mislabeled as lukewarm or weak. This is not a middle road—it is a narrow road. It is difficult to walk. It often doesn't make sense. The only way to get across is to tie ourselves to Jesus and follow him closely.

It is possible that being tied to this man will make you unpopular or even cost you your life. But I also believe it is the only way to truly find your life. And if it means I can receive his life, real life that does not end, popularity is something I am willing to trade.

ACKNOWLEDGMENTS

Father, Son, and Holy Spirit: Thank you for saving and adopting me. Thank you for giving me life. Thank you for all of the people listed below and all the others who have shaped my story. And thank you for everything else there is that is worth being thankful for.

Heather: Thank you for plucking the pages of this manuscript out of the fire, blowing off the embers, and helping me tape the pieces back together. If you had not done this, I would have quit. Thank you for the thousand hours you gave to allow me time to write. Thank you for showing me the places my words needed to be softer or simpler. Thank you for being the reason I was able to finish writing a book—something I have dreamed of since I was five. Thank you for loving me.

Samuel, Noah, Eliana (and JJ and Ezra who were born after this book was first published): Thank you for being my kids. And thank you for reminding me that it is not possible to see God unless I learn to look for him with the eyes of a child.

Melinda, Grandma Marian, and Aunt Lois: Thank you for praying.

Eric and David: Thank you for reading.

Blair: Thank you for telling me that I am a writer.

Morgan: Thank you for showing me the door was not locked.

NOTES

Introduction

1. Christian Smith, *Christian America?: What Evangelicals Really Want* (Los Angeles: University of California Press, 2000), inside cover and 5.

2. Lee Strobel, *The Case for the Real Jesus: A Journalistic Investigates Current Attacks on the Identity of Christ* (Grand Rapids, MI: Zondervan, 2007), 10–11.

3. David Kinnaman, *UnChristian: What a new generation really thinks about Christianity … and why it matters* (Grand Rapids, MI: Baker Books, 2007), 15.

4. Sam Harris, *Letter to a Christian Nation* (New York: Alfred A. Knopf, 2006), 8, xii.

5. Strobel, *The Case for the Real Jesus*, 20.

6. Kinnaman, *UnChristian*, 27.

7. Ibid, 26.

8. Harris, *Letter to a Christian Nation*, 70.

9. Strobel, *The Case for the Real Jesus*, 11.

10. Donald Miller, *A Million Miles in a Thousand Years: How I learned to live a better story* (Nashville: Thomas Nelson, 2009), 117.

11. John Shelby Spong, *Why Christianity Must Change or Die: A Bishop Speaks to Believers in Exile* (San Francisco: Harper, 1998), inside cover.

12. Harris, *Letter to a Christian Nation*, vii.

Chapter 1

1. "Who Is Terry Jones? Pastor Behind 'Burn a Koran Day'," *ABC News*, accessed on 12/16/2010, http:abcnews.go.com/US/terry-jones-pastor-burn-koran-day/story?id=11575665.

2. "Rudolph, unsorry, gets life for abortion clinic bombing," *USA Today*, accessed on 12/16/2010, http://www.usatoday.com/news/nation/2005-07-17-rudolph-monday-sentencing_x.htm

3. "Nepal: Hindus Threaten Bombings," *Voice of the Martyrs*, last modified June 2, 2009, accessed November 13, 2010, http://www.persecution.com/public/newsroomprint.aspx?story_ID=MTQw.

4. Mosab Hassan Yousef with Ron Brackin, *Son of Hamas: A Gripping Account of Terror, Betrayal, Political Intrigue, and Unthinkable Choices* (Tyndale, 2010), 2.

5. Benjamin Wiker, *10 Books that Screwed Up the World: And 5 Others that Didn't Help* (New York: MJF Books, 2008), 118.

Chapter 2

1. Martha Sherrill, "Welcome to the Banquet," *O, The Oprah Magazine*, vol. 9, number 5, May 2008, 281.

2. Ravi Zacharias, *Jesus Among Other Gods: The Absolute Claims of the Christian Message* (W Publishing Group, 2000), 54.

Chapter 3

1. Matthew 5:44
2. Matthew 5:39–40
3. Luke 23:34
4. "Mount Gerizim," *Wikipedia*, last modified January 17, 2012, accessed March 22, 2012, http://en.wikipedia.org/wiki/Mount_Gerizim.
5. John 4:19–24
6. Luke 10:30–35
7. Luke 17:11–19
8. Mosab Hassan Yousef, *Son of Hamas: A Gripping Account of Terror, Betrayal, Political Intrigue and Unthinkable Choices* (Salt River, 2010), 18–22.
9. Ibid, 228.
10. Matthew 5:31–32
11. Matthew 5:27–29
12. John 7:53–8:11
13. C.S. Lewis, *The Problem of Pain* (New York: Harper One, 1940), 49.

Chapter 4

1. Timothy Keller, *The Reason for God* (New York: Riverhead Books, 2008), 8.

Part II

1. Exodus 16

Chapter 5

1. Genesis 1–2
2. Ibid

3. David Berlinski, "What Brings a World into Being," *Commentary* (March 31, 2001): accessed online on 02/22/2009 through http://www.discovery.org/a/616.

4. John 9:1–7

5. Matthew 20:29–34

6. Mark 10:50–52 and Luke 18:35–43

7. Angus Buchan, *Faith like Potatoes*, directed by Reghardt van den Bergh (Affirm Films, Sony Pictures), DVD.

Chapter 6

1. Charles Darwin, *The Origin of Species & The Descent of Man* (New York: Modern Library), 521.

2. Quoted in Janet Browne, *Charles Darwin: The Power of Place* (Princeton University Press, 2002), 85.

3. Michael Shermer, *Why Darwin Matters: The Case Against Intelligent Design* (New York: Times Books, 2006), 50.

4. Ibid, 152–153.

5. Ben Stein, *Expelled: No Intelligence Allowed*, directed by Nathan Frankowski (Universal City, CA: Vivendi Entertainment, 2008), DVD.

6. J. P. Moreland, *Scaling the Secular City: A Defense of Christianity* (Grand Rapids, MI: Baker Books, 1987), 20.

7. David Berlinski, "Was There a Big Bang," *Commentary* (February 1998): 32.

8. Edgar Andrews, *Who Made God: Searching for a Theory of Everything* (England: EP Books, 2009), 101.

9. Berlinski, "Was there a Big Bang," 33.

10. Hugh Ross, *Creator and the Cosmos: How the Greatest Scientific Discoveries of the Century Reveal God* (Colorado Springs, CO: Navpress, 1995), 64.

11. Berlinski, "Was there a Big Bang," 38.

12. G.K. Chesterton, *Orthodoxy* (New York: Dodd, Mead & Co, 1908), 11.

Chapter 7

1. John 8:23

2. Philippians 2:5–7

3. Mark 8:22–25

4. John 6:15

5. Luke 2:41–47

6. Matthew 13:53–57
7. Matthew 22:41–46
8. John 1
9. Job 38
10. John 8:28
11. Matthew 24:36
12. Matthew 7:7–8
13. G. K. Chesterton, *Orthodoxy* (New York: Dodd, Mead & Co, 1908), 23.
14. James 4:6
15. Isaiah 5:21
16. Matthew 11:25
17. John 1:14, Colossians 1:15

Chapter 8

1. A.W. Tozer, *The Pursuit of God* (SoHo Books), 30.
2. J. Craig Ventor, "J. Craig Ventor: Designing Life," *60 Minutes* (CBS News, 2010), accessed online on 03/23/2012 through http://www.cbsnews.com/video/watch/?id=7076435n.

Chapter 9

1. Joan Winmill Brown, *The Martyred Christian: 160 Readings from Dietrich Bonhoeffer* (New York: Macmillan Publishing Co. Inc., 1983), xiv–xv.

Chapter 10

1. Ravi Zacharias, *Jesus Among Other Gods: The Absolute Claims of the Christian Message* (W Publishing Group), 115.
2. Benjamin Wiker, *The Darwin Myth: The Life and Lies of Charles Darwin* (Washington, DC: Regnery Publishing, 2009), 118.
3. "You Know It's a Myth," *American Atheists*, accessed on 12/16/2010, https://atheists.org/atheism/Christmas.
4. Ravi Zacharias, *Jesus Among Other Gods: The Absolute Claims of the Christian Message* (W Publishing Group, 2000), 121. (Chandogya Upanishad 5.10.8)
5. From Angutarra Nikaya, 7.5, quoted in *Guide to the Tipitaka* (Bangkok: White Lotus Company, Ltd., 1993), 97.
6. Sumbul Ali-Karamali, *The Muslim Next Door: The Qur'an, the Media and that Veil*

NOTES

Thing (Ashland, OR: White Cloud Press, 2008), 19.

7. David Ariel, *What Do Jews Believe: The Spiritual Foundations of Judaism* (New York: Schocken Books, 1995), 85.

8. Abraham Cohen, *Every Man's Talmud: The Major Teachings of the Rabbinic Sages* (New York: Schocken Books, 1949), 88.

9. Psalm 14:3

10. Romans 3:23

11. Mark 10:18

12. Genesis 3

13. Ephesians 6:12

14. John 10:10

Chapter 11

1. Lee Strobel, *The Case for Faith: A Journalist Investigates the Toughest Objections to Christianity* (Grand Rapids, MI: Zondervan, 2000), 31.

2. Isaiah 53:5

3. John 12:1–8

4. Luke 22:41–46

5. John 18:11 and Luke 22:51

6. John 11:23–26

7. "Former Washington state man saves wife's life during AZ shooting," *MyNorthwest*, accessed on 02/24/2011, http://www.mynorthwest.com/?nid=189&sid=411330.

8. John 3:4–7

9. John 14:16–18

10. Romans 8:11

Chapter 12

1. Ziauddin Sardar, *What Do Muslims Believe: The Roots and Realities of Modern Islam* (New York: Walker & Company, 2007), 46, 77.

2. David Ariel, *What Do Jews Believe: The Spiritual Foundations of Judaism* (New York: Schocken Books, 1995), 245–246.

3. Psalm 89:48

4. G. K. Chesterton, *Orthodoxy* (New York: Dodd, Mead & Co, 1908), 14.

5. Joan Winmill Brown, *The Martyred Christian: 160 Readings from Dietrich Bonhoeffer* (New York: Macmillan Publishing Co. Inc., 1983), xviii.

www.ingramcontent.com/pod-product-compliance
Lightning Source LLC
LaVergne TN
LVHW041545070426
835507LV00011B/929